101 BEST LOVED

CHOCOLATE RECIPES

Consultant Editor
Jane Suthering

HOTEL
Chocolat.

First published in 2007 by

Hotel Chocolat Limited
Mint House
Royston
SG8 5HL
England

website: www.hotelchocolat.co.uk

ISBN 978-0-9557052-1-2

Printed and bound in Portugal by Printer Portuguesa Lda

Book creation by Elephant Book Company Limited
Consultant: Jane Suthering
Editor: Janet Illsley
Page makeup: Graham Beehag
Commissioned photography: Vanessa Courtier
Index: Sandra Shotter

For Hotel Chocolat
Publisher: Terry Waters
Creative Director: Fredrik Ahlin
Design: Kat Kannegieter
Copy: Simon Thirlwell
Photographer: Stephen Bond

COOK'S NOTES

• All spoon measures are level unless otherwise stated: 1 tsp = 5ml; 1 tbsp = 15ml.

• Use medium eggs unless otherwise suggested – preferably organic or free-range.

• Anyone who is pregnant or in a vulnerable health group should avoid those recipes within this book that contain raw egg whites or lightly cooked eggs.

• Use unwaxed fruit, whenever possible, if a recipe calls for the zest to be used. Always wash other citrus fruit thoroughly before use.

• Use fresh rather than dried herbs unless otherwise listed.

• Make sure eggs, butter and all other ingredients are at room temperature before you start a recipe.

• Oven timings given in the recipes apply to conventional ovens. If you are using a fan-assisted oven, lower the oven setting by 15–20°C (1 Gas Mark) and check before the end of the suggested cooking time.

• Timings are provided as a guide, along with a description of colour or texture as appropriate, but ovens vary and readers must rely on their own judgement as to when a cake or other dish is properly cooked.

Foreword

An enduring love affair that has lasted 3,500 years and is still growing stronger: the human being and the cocoa bean really seem to like each other. We love the taste and the bean obliges by imparting health-giving benefits worthy of its superfood status.

Imagine then the metaphorical place that is Hotel Chocolat brought real. A place where every delectable morsel served through the day has chocolate within it. Welcome to these pages – from morning to midnight, savoury and sweet recipes to excite and delight you.

Bon appétit

Angus

Angus Thirlwell, co-founder of Hotel Chocolat

This book is all about indulgence – if that's what you want to call it – or simply enjoying the delights of one of the most exciting ingredients in the cook's repertoire. Chocolate is no longer something you just throw into your supermarket trolley. Today it is produced by specialist chocolatiers sourcing quality cocoa beans from the diverse growing regions around the world, each with its own distinctive characteristics.

You can, for example, now buy a milk chocolate with 50 per cent cocoa solids that is quite unlike any milk chocolate bar traditionally enjoyed by the British palate; a chocolate (with 70 per cent cocoa solids) made from Cuban Trinitario beans, which lend wine and leather notes; a chocolate from Peru (with 64 per cent cocoa solids) that has undertones of dried fruit; or a range of 'Single Estate' chocolate bars. Chocolate is now talked about with the kind of knowledge and reverence associated with fine wine, and a terminology comparable to the world of wine has been adopted.

So why not start a 'journey of discovery', by tasting the different varieties of chocolate at leisure and finding out which are your particular favourites? It can only enhance your enjoyment of the tempting recipes in this book. Chosen by some of the best-known cookery writers and chefs, each and every one is a favourite.

As an anonymous wag once wrote – 'there's more to life than chocolate … but not right now!'

Pleasure or health?

One of the many pleasures of chocolate comes from its unique property of melting at body heat. Let it melt on your tongue and it will soften into a warm, comforting liquid. Sense the tastes and aromas it releases. How could it not be good for us? Indeed, the health-giving benefits of chocolate have been recognised for centuries.

Cocoa has long been associated with medical remedies. Native Americans used it to cure sickness and it was alleged to cure itches, prevent tumours and encourage sleep. By the 1680s it was thought that chocolate could restore energy after a hard day's work, help prevent lung infections and strengthen the heart.

Continuing research offers all sorts of potential 'health' properties of cocoa and fine chocolate:

- Cocoa butter, the naturally occurring fat in cocoa beans, is a mixture of saturated, unsaturated and monounsaturated, but it is mainly unsaturated fat, commonly called 'good' fat as it helps raise HDL cholesterol and so protects the heart.
- Dark chocolate is high in minerals – magnesium, phosphorus, potassium, copper, iron and calcium – essential for good health.
- Dark chocolate is high on the list of antioxidant foods – both in terms of quality and quantity. Antioxidants are credited with diffusing free radicals in the body, helping to protect against the destruction of body cells, thereby potentially assisting to regulate blood pressure, prevent heart disease and reduce the risk of cancer. They have also been associated with reducing inflammation around the joints, so easing arthritic pain.
- Naturally occurring 'chemicals' in the cocoa bean stimulate the brain in the same way as caffeine or adrenaline, giving a burst of energy. They also affect the brain's mood centres evoking happiness and that 'feel-good' factor.

- And if these benefits aren't enough, you can indulge in spa treatments including 'chocolate massage' and 'cocoa nib exfoliation' to leave your skin feeling wonderful!

Food of the Gods

The botanical name for the cocoa tree is Theobroma Cacao, theobroma meaning 'food of the gods'. If, indeed, cocoa is the food of the gods then Heaven exists on Earth in a limited location. With few exceptions, this extraordinary tree only bears fruit within a band of 20° either side of the Equator. Hotel Chocolat's very own estate, Rabot, is situated on the edge of The Pitons National Park, a World Heritage site, on the Caribbean island of St. Lucia.

Cocoa is an unusual tree – the cocoa pod begins life as a tiny white flower emerging directly from the trunk and lower branches, gradually ripening and swelling to form large pods. These contain 30–40 seeds or 'beans' cushioned in a white pulp.

There are three major varieties of bean – Criollo, Forastro and Trinitario, each with its own distinctive tastes. Nothing in the world has such complex flavours and aromas – over 300 chemical compounds and 400 aromas have been identified in the cocoa bean! Many of these chemical compounds are similar or identical to those found in other foods, which is why it's easy to associate such tastes as berry fruit, apple, wine, honey or herbs in chocolate.

How chocolate is produced

Exactly how are humble cocoa beans transformed into the chocolate that beckons so enticingly? Chocolate is a mixture of cocoa mass, cocoa butter and sugar, often with the addition of milk and a variety of flavourings. Creating it is a painstaking, time-consuming and laborious process, which starts with the growers. Their job does not end with nurturing these notoriously delicate trees, nor with the equally strenuous process of manually harvesting the pods. How they treat the cocoa beans after harvesting is crucial to the quality of the finished product.

The precise nature of the process varies from country to country but it goes something like this. The pods are sliced open to reveal their cargo of fleshy white fruit. The wet beans and pulp are piled onto palm leaves and covered with more leaves, or they are put in specially made wooden boxes, to undergo the fermentation process.

Fermentation

The beans and pulp are allowed to ferment or sweat for an average of 4 to 7 days, depending on the type of bean. The temperature climbs to about 60°C, which liquefies and drains off the pulp, softening too the bitterness of the fresh beans. The heat causes a chemical change in which the natural sugars are converted to lactic and acetic acid and also activates enzymes in the beans. This process develops the characteristic chocolate flavour notes, similar to the fermentation of grapes in wine making.

Drying

The next step is drying, best done naturally in the open air. In some areas, where there is unpredictable rainfall and a danger of the damp causing mould growth, the beans will be dried over open fires. But that in its turn gives rise to the danger of flavour contamination. The smoky taste can be so pervasive that it can ruin a whole batch of chocolate.

The beans are spread out to dry in the sun for 1 to 2 weeks. Every few days they are raked and turned to ensure even drying. This brings the water content right down, from 80 per cent humidity to about 5 to 7 per cent. The beans, whose weight has dropped to a quarter of the harvest weight, are packed into large hessian sacks ready to be sold and then made into chocolate.

Because the vast bulk of world chocolate production is concentrated in the hands of a few conglomerates, only a handful of specialist producers like Hotel Chocolat can make single-estate chocolate where the provenance of the bean is kept intact. Hotel Chocolat is able to source the best possible beans, whether grown on its own St. Lucia plantation or bought from small producers elsewhere in the West Indies.

Once the beans are ready to be made into chocolate, the real magic begins. The beans are carefully checked and sorted. They are sometimes dried again to remove any residual moisture. This makes winnowing, the separation of the cocoa nib or inner seed from the shell, easier.

Roasting

The nibs are roasted, a delicate process crucial to the flavour and colour of the final chocolate. They are cooked inside a rotating cylinder at a temperature of 120 to 140°C, losing another 10 per cent of their original weight. Each batch of beans to be used in a particular type of chocolate gets roasted separately. The beans can be blended, as with wine or malt whisky, and good quality blends do exist. However, the big brands will often opt for blending to produce a consistent and arguably blander 'house taste'.

Single origin refers to beans from a single country, such as Cuba, Java or Ghana. The result is usually good quality chocolate, which is beginning to allow the flavour of the cocoa beans shine through.

Single estate refers to beans from a single, named estate. This lets the personality of the beans really

sing out. The beans have a pure taste unique to their terroir (the soil and conditions they were grown in). Hotel Chocolat makes a single estate chocolate from the beans grown on its St. Lucia plantation.

Grinding and refining

Originally the beans were stone ground, but these days metal mills with sophisticated temperature controls are used. The nibs are ground by passing them through a series of rollers. This produces a liquid paste, known as cocoa mass or cocoa liquor, which contains around 55 per cent cocoa butter.

Mixing

The cocoa mass goes into a mixer with sugar, extra cocoa butter and sometimes milk (for milk chocolate recipes). Deciding how much sugar to add to the blend is one of the greatest skills in chocolate making. Sugar is much cheaper than cocoa, which is why so much mass-produced chocolate is sickly sweet, and why real chocolate is correspondingly more expensive. Excessive sugar

is also used to mask poor quality chocolate made with low-grade cocoa and other money-saving ingredients – for example, vegetable fat instead of cocoa butter.

The mixture is beaten until it becomes a smooth paste called a 'dough'. The dough is refined through steel rollers, which pulverise the individual particles until they are reduced in size. The smaller the particle, the smoother the finished chocolate will taste. But at this stage it is still gritty.

Conching

To make it taste entirely smooth and silky, the mixture now has to be conched, a process named after the original shell-shaped vessel invented in 1880 by Rudolph Lindt. The machine's arms work the chocolate back and forth at a range of temperatures between 5 to 85°C, kneading the chocolate mixture to a liquid texture, finessing the particle size to an extremely fine 18 to 20 microns. During the conching the flavour is further developed, free radicals are vaporised reducing

bitterness, the moisture content is lowered and more fat is squeezed out of the cocoa particles. Towards the end of conching, any desired flavourings, such as vanilla, are added.

Conching can go on for anywhere between 12 and 72 hours. In general, the longer the conching time, the better the resulting chocolate will be. The exception is premium, single-estate cocoa. Many producers are now using a shortened conching time so that the full personality of these premium cocoa beans is retained.

Tempering

Tempering is a precisely calibrated cooling technique that encourages the fine, stable crystallisation of the cocoa butter and its even dispersal through the chocolate. It ensures a chocolate with a good, clean snap, an attractive sheen and good keeping qualities. It is now ready to be moulded into chocolate bars or used as couverture (the French word for covering) for individual chocolates.

These are the basic processes that turn the lowly cocoa bean into chocolate, producing the chocolate maker's basic ingredients. It should be noted that with very few exceptions, the making of chocolate from the bean has become concentrated in the hands of a few multinationals. Hotel Chocolat is the only UK chocolate company to make its own chocolate from scratch with beans grown on its own cocoa estate. Other European countries can perhaps boast rather more than a handful apiece. But most chocolate makers now buy their couverture ready-made from specialist multinational suppliers. These trade suppliers offer an enormous range of couvertures — from the lowest-grade artificial chocolate (called chocolate compound), right up to excellent quality, single-origin chocolate. Which couverture a chocolatier chooses to buy very much defines their place in the overall quality pecking order.

Working with chocolate

Chocolate is relatively easy to use in cooking, but it is a complex ingredient and must be treated with respect. It is particularly sensitive to heat and care needs to be taken when melting it or combining melted chocolate with other ingredients. For the same reason, you need a cool working environment when you are making chocolate decorations, otherwise they are liable to melt!

Melting chocolate

First, break the chocolate into even-sized pieces so that it can melt smoothly. Place the pieces of chocolate in a small heatproof bowl and stand this in a metal sieve or colander set over a saucepan of simmering water – this way the bowl will not touch the water and get too hot. Warm it just until the chocolate melts, stirring occasionally with a plastic spatula or spoon. As soon as the chocolate is melted and smooth, remove the bowl from the pan of water.

Alternatively, chocolate may be melted in the microwave on medium. Timing will vary according to the amount of chocolate used and the power of your microwave setting. Take a look at your microwave manufacturer's booklet for guidelines before you start.

As a general guide, break up the chocolate into a glass or plastic bowl and microwave on medium for 1 minute. Then check the consistency by touching it with a fingertip or a plastic spatula. (Chocolate can be deceptive as it often keeps its form even when it's almost melted.) Return the bowl to the microwave for another 30 seconds and then test it again. Do this until the chocolate is melted.

Remember that chocolate has a tendency to become overheated quickly. If this happens it is liable to 'seize' into a solid lump and there is no remedy for this. So, watch it carefully – especially white chocolate, which is particularly sensitive.

Chocolate decorations

The first few attempts at chocolate decorations can be very frustrating, but practice makes perfect. Different kinds of chocolate behave differently once melted. Cheap cake coverings, for example, make great curls, but the taste is inferior to a good quality chocolate. The latter can be brittle and may splinter as you try to scrape it off a surface to make the curls if the chocolate has set too hard.

Fortunately, all chocolate can be piped very successfully once it has cooled and thickened to a suitable consistency.

Piping chocolate

For a simple yet effective drizzled finish to a cake or dessert, spoon some melted, cooled chocolate into a small greaseproof paper piping bag. Snip off the end and drizzle an abstract pattern straight onto the finished confection. This is particularly effective if you aim for a contrasting effect, such as piping white chocolate onto a dark chocolate covered cake. You can also feather the chocolate once you've piped it, provided the covering is still soft, by swirling the piped chocolate with the tip of a cocktail stick.

Chocolate shavings

Pull a potato peeler evenly across the surface of a bar of chocolate at room temperature to produce shavings. (If the chocolate is chilled, the shavings will shatter.)

Alternatively, spread melted chocolate in a thin layer on a marble slab or other smooth surface and leave until only just set. Scrape shavings from the chocolate by holding the blade of a knife at an oblique angle and pushing it across the chocolate. Store chocolate shavings in an airtight container in a cool place (the fridge if necessary).

Chocolate shapes

Spread melted chocolate evenly on a sheet of baking parchment secured on a tray. Tap the tray firmly on a work surface to level the chocolate. Leave to cool until just set but not hard, then stamp out shapes with a cutter, or cut geometric shapes with a sharp knife.

Using a palette knife, carefully transfer the shapes to a tray and leave them to set hard. Store in an airtight container in a cool place (the fridge if necessary), layered between sheets of baking parchment. They will last for a few weeks.

Chocolate ganache

This was created by accident when a clumsy apprentice in a Parisian pastry shop knocked some boiling cream into a tub of chocolate. The patissier called him *un ganache* (an imbecile) then later realised he had inadvertently created something special – hence the name, ganache. It can be used in many ways: poured over cakes to give a glossy coating; as a sauce with a dash of alcohol added, such as brandy or whisky; to make truffles; and on cooling it can be used for decorative piping, or for a textured icing.

To make ganache, break 225g good quality dark chocolate into small pieces and place in a small bowl. Heat 150ml double cream to just scalding (almost boiling) and pour onto the chocolate, stirring all the time. When the chocolate is almost melted, work in 25g unsalted butter until you a have a rich glossy sauce. Keep warm or use as required.

For a slightly sweetened ganache, blend a little soft light brown sugar into the cream in the early stages of heating.

Chocolate sauce

This is perfect for poached pears, ice cream or a classic banana split. It will keep, covered, in the fridge for up to a week.

Break 250g dark chocolate into small pieces and place in a small saucepan with 200ml cold water and 75g caster sugar. Heat slowly, stirring, until the chocolate is melted and smooth, then simmer gently for about 5 minutes, stirring occasionally, until it has a rich sauce consistency. Remove from the heat and stir in 2 tbsp softened butter and 4 tbsp double cream.

Vanilla sugar

Some chocolate recipes call for vanilla sugar, which is easy to make yourself. Simply keep one or two dry vanilla pods – split, or even spent (with their seeds scraped out) – in a jar of caster sugar sealed with a tight-fitting lid. The vanilla fragrance and flavour will infuse the sugar. Top up the sugar as you use it and add empty vanilla pods as they become available.

Sugar syrup

For some chocolate mousses and a few other recipes in this book, you'll need a sugar syrup. You may only use a small quantity but the rest will keep in the fridge, covered, for up to 2 weeks.

To make a light sugar syrup, dissolve 125g granulated sugar in 300ml water in a small saucepan over a low heat. Once dissolved, add 1 tbsp lemon juice, if you like. Bring to the boil, then cool and strain.

To make a heavier sugar syrup, suitable for ice creams and sorbets, use double the amount of sugar.

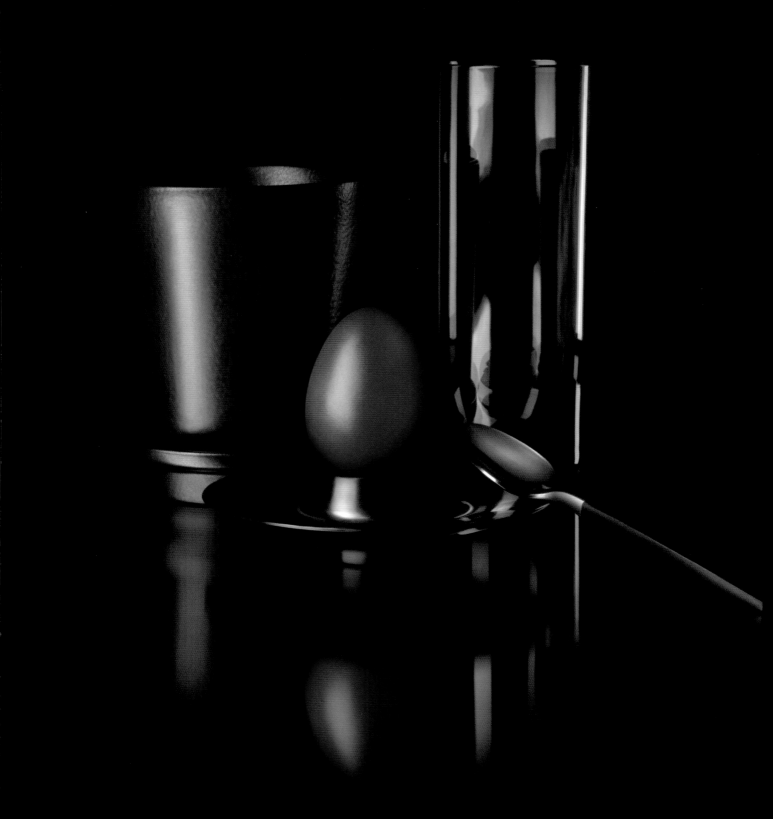

Breakfast

Whether it's a late and lazy weekend or an early morning wake-up call, breakfast is one of the first things on our minds. And with the help of these stirring recipes, from cloud-like muffins and long, languid churros to the exciting crunch of granola, you'll be feeding both body and soul. Wake up and smell the chocolate.

Jane Suthering's
Chocolate Granola

MAKES ABOUT 900g

400g porridge oats
115g oat bran and oat germ
115g light muscovado sugar
115g assorted nuts, chopped
55g desiccated coconut
85g sunflower seeds
30g sesame seeds
150ml vegetable oil
150ml water
2 tbsp cocoa powder, sifted

½ tsp vanilla extract
½ tsp salt
115–225g milk or dark
   chocolate, chopped

To SERVE:
milk or yogurt
fruit, such as berries or bananas
   (optional)

Preheat the oven to 200°C/Gas 6. In a large bowl, combine the oats, oat bran and oat germ, sugar, chopped nuts, coconut and seeds.

In another bowl, whisk together the oil, water, cocoa powder, vanilla extract and salt until well combined. Stir this into the dry ingredients in the other bowl and mix thoroughly.

Transfer the mixture to two large baking trays and spread out evenly. Bake for 15 minutes, then stir and turn the mixture thoroughly on the trays and bake for a further 15 minutes.

Allow to cool on the trays, then mix in the chopped chocolate. Store in an airtight container and use as required.

Serve with milk or yogurt and fresh fruit, such as raspberries, blueberries, bananas or strawberries, if you like.

Crunchy breakfast
cereal is a great way to start the day. Make this one in batches and store it in an airtight container. Serve with milk, or natural yogurt and fresh fruit if you wish.

Felicity Barnum-Bobb's
Chocolate Brownie Muffins

MAKES 12

350g dark (but not bitter)
   chocolate, in pieces
175g butter
100g self-raising flour

225g golden caster sugar
3 tbsp milk
3 medium eggs

Preheat the oven to 190°C/Gas 5. Line a 12-hole muffin tin with paper muffin cases. Melt the chocolate and butter together in a bowl over a pan of simmering water (or microwave on medium for 2 minutes, stir, then microwave on high for a further 2 minutes, or until just melted). Let cool slightly.

Sift the flour into a bowl and stir in the sugar. Add the milk and eggs to the melted chocolate and mix together, then pour into the dry ingredients and stir together until just combined.

Spoon the mixture into the cases and bake for 20 minutes until risen and just firm. Transfer to a wire rack to cool slightly. Serve warm.

Wicked fudgey centres make these brownie muffins hugely appealing. It's the seriously large quantity of chocolate used that gives them their gooey texture. Use a medium dark chocolate with about 50% cocoa solids, rather than one with a high percentage of cocoa solids, which makes the brownies too bitter in my view.

Packed with energy and fibre, these chunky nut and oat bars are ideal for a quick breakfast on the run. Use almonds rather than hazelnuts if you prefer.

Christine France's
Breakfast Bars
with chocolate and hazelnuts

MAKES 12

115g unsalted butter, plus extra to grease
75g light muscovado sugar
30ml golden syrup
175g rolled oats
45g blanched hazelnuts, roughly chopped

45g ready-to-eat dried apricots, roughly chopped
1 tsp vanilla extract
80g dark chocolate, roughly chopped

Preheat the oven to 180°C/Gas 4. Lightly grease a shallow 18 x 28cm cake tin and line the base with baking parchment.

Place the butter, sugar and golden syrup in a large pan and stir over a low heat until just melted. Remove from the heat and stir in the oats, hazelnuts, apricots and vanilla, then finally add the chocolate, stirring to mix evenly.

Spoon the mixture into the prepared tin and smooth the top level. Bake for 20–25 minutes, or until golden brown and firm.

Leave to cool in the tin. After about 10 minutes, cut into 12 bars. Turn out of the tin when cold.

Jacque Malouf's
Churros with Chocolate

SERVES 4

CHURROS:
90g caster sugar
1 tsp ground cinnamon
400ml water
200g strong plain flour
¼ tsp salt
1 large egg
vegetable oil, to deep-fry

HOT CHOCOLATE:
500ml milk
120g dark chocolate, chopped
  or grated
1 tsp cornflour
1 tbsp caster sugar, or to taste

For the churros, mix the caster sugar and cinnamon together and scatter on a large serving plate.

Bring the water to a rolling boil in a pan set over a high heat. Add the flour and salt, take off the heat and beat vigorously with a wooden spoon for about 1 minute until the flour is absorbed. Don't expect a smooth mixture – it will be pasty, a little like gloopy mashed potato.

Set aside to cool for 15 minutes, then beat in the egg. At first it will seem as if the egg will not incorporate into the mixture but it just takes a little perseverance.

Heat the oil in a large heavy-based pan or deep-fryer. Put the dough into a large, strong piping bag, fitted with a fluted nozzle. You will need to fry the churros in about 3 batches, as follows:

Carefully squeeze out the dough (it will be quite firm) directly over the hot oil, cutting it into 15–20cm lengths with scissors. Allow the strips to fall into the oil (but not from too much of a height, to avoid splashing). Cook about 4 churros at a time for 3–4 minutes, turning once until they are golden brown. Drain on kitchen paper. Repeat with the remaining mixture to make about 12 churros in total. Roll them in the cinnamon sugar and keep warm.

For the chocolate, warm the milk in a pan set over a medium heat. Add the chocolate and stir until melted. In a small bowl, mix the cornflour with 2 tbsp of the hot chocolate to a smooth paste. Pour the mixture back into the pan, whisking well. Cook for 4–5 minutes, stirring often, until the chocolate is the thickness of double cream. Sweeten with sugar to taste.

Pour the hot chocolate into 4 small heatproof cups and serve with the warm churros for dipping.

Churros with hot chocolate is a popular breakfast or mid-morning snack throughout Spain. For best results, use a regular sweet dark chocolate, rather than a bitter one.

Good Housekeeping's
Hot Chocolate Sandwiches
with banana and toffee

SERVES 4

8 thick slices of white bread
4 tbsp Very Lazy Sticky Toffee
    Sauce (English Provender
    Company)

2 bananas, sliced
50g dark chocolate, grated
25g butter
golden caster sugar, to sprinkle

Spread half the slices of bread with the toffee sauce and divide the banana slices and chocolate between them. Sandwich together with the other bread slices.

Melt half the butter in a large frying pan and fry the sandwiches, in batches if necessary, for 4–5 minutes on each side until golden, adding more butter once you've turned them over.

Sprinkle the sandwiches with a little sugar while they are still hot. Serve immediately.

Fried sandwiches with an oozing chocolate and toffee banana filling…pure indulgence.

Resembling the *pain au chocolat* of pre-World War II France, these rolls are simply basic bread dough baked around some good couverture chocolate – unlike today's chocolate-filled croissant dough. They are best eaten freshly baked and warm for breakfast, but any that are leftover can be reheated in a microwave the following day.

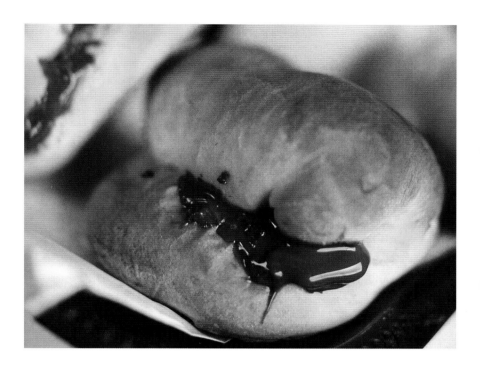

Sue Lawrence's
Chocolate Bread Rolls

MAKES 10

625g strong white bread flour, plus extra to dust
2 tsp salt
1 sachet easy-blend dried yeast
30g butter, cut into cubes
30g caster sugar

about 340ml semi-skimmed milk, warmed, plus extra to glaze
110–140g dark chocolate (50–60% cocoa solids) or good quality milk chocolate, chopped

Combine the flour, salt and yeast in a large bowl. Rub in the butter, then stir in the sugar and make a well in the centre. Add enough warm milk to mix to a fairly stiff dough. Turn onto a floured board and knead for about 10 minutes. Place in an oiled bowl, cover tightly with cling film and leave to prove in the fridge overnight.

The next morning, knock back the dough with your fists, then divide into 10 pieces. Roll each into a rectangle, about 10 x 15cm. Place the chopped chocolate down the middle, then roll up like a Swiss-roll, tucking in the ends. Place on a baking tray, cover loosely and leave to rise in a warm place for about 30–40 minutes.

Preheat the oven to 220°C/Gas 7. Uncover the rolls, brush with milk and bake for about 15 minutes until risen and golden brown. Cool on a wire rack for about 5 minutes. Serve warm.

Eric Treuille and Ursula Ferrigno's
Prune and Chocolate Bread

MAKES 1 LOAF

2½ tsp dried yeast
350ml water
500g strong white bread flour,
 plus extra to dust
1½ tsp salt
30g unsalted butter, softened, plus
 extra to grease tin

375g pitted prunes, roughly
 chopped
375g plain chocolate, roughly
 chopped
1 egg, beaten

Sprinkle the yeast into 100ml of the water in a small bowl. Leave for 5 minutes, then stir to dissolve.

Sift the flour and salt together into a large bowl. Make a well in the centre and pour in the yeasted water. Gradually mix in the flour, adding as much of the remaining water as needed to form a soft, sticky dough.

Turn the dough out onto a lightly floured work surface and knead until smooth and elastic, about 10 minutes. Put the dough in a clean bowl and cover with a tea-towel. Leave to rise until doubled in size, about 1 hour. Grease a 1kg loaf tin with softened butter.

Knock back the dough, then leave to rest for 10 minutes. Now incorporate the prunes, chocolate, butter, and egg, using your hands to gently squeeze these ingredients into the dough until evenly distributed and the egg is absorbed. Turn out onto a lightly floured work surface and knead until just firm enough to shape, 1–2 minutes.

To shape the dough, gently roll it backwards and forwards until it is the same length as the tin and an even thickness. Tuck under the ends and place in the prepared tin, seam-side down. Cover with a tea-towel and leave to prove until the dough has risen to 2.5cm above the rim of the tin, about 30 minutes. Preheat the oven to 180°C/Gas 4.

Bake the loaf in the oven for 45 minutes or until it is lightly browned and sounds hollow when tapped on the underside with your knuckles. Turn out onto a wire rack and leave to cool.

Deeply indulgent and chock-a-block with juicy prunes and chocolate, this loaf is superb served warm, cut into thick slices. The chocolate and prunes are roughly chopped so that the bread is packed with large chunks of flavour. Serve for breakfast, or as a treat with mid-morning coffee or afternoon tea.

Richard Bertinet's
Chocolate Buns

MAKES 24

DOUGH:
250ml full-fat milk
500g strong white bread flour,
   plus extra to dust
15g fresh yeast (or 7g easy-blend
   dried yeast)
60g unsalted butter
40g caster sugar
10g salt
2 large eggs
25g cocoa powder

CHOCOLATE PASTRY CREAM:
6 egg yolks
140g caster sugar
50g plain flour, sifted
500ml full-fat milk
15g cocoa powder
15g butter, cut into flakes

TO ASSEMBLE:
200g chocolate chips (milk, dark
   or a mixture)
egg wash (2 eggs beaten with a
   pinch of salt)

To make the dough, warm the milk in a pan to body temperature (it should feel neither warm nor cold when you dip your finger into it). Put the flour in a large bowl and rub in the yeast using your fingertips (as if making a crumble). Rub in the butter, then stir in the sugar and salt. Now add the eggs, milk and cocoa powder and work the ingredients together by hand (or in a mixer) until you have a smooth dough. Cover with a clean tea-towel and leave to rise for 45 minutes in a warm, draught-free place.

Meanwhile, make the chocolate pastry cream. Whisk the egg yolks, half the sugar and all the flour together in a bowl until smooth. Put the remaining sugar in a heavy-based pan with the milk and cocoa powder and place over a low heat until it almost reaches a simmer. Slowly pour a third of the milk onto the egg mixture, whisking constantly, then add the remaining milk and stir again. Pour back into the pan and slowly bring to the boil, stirring. Simmer for a couple of minutes, stirring constantly. Pour into a dish to cool and dot the surface with flakes of butter to prevent a skin forming.

To shape the buns, transfer the dough to a lightly floured surface and gently flatten with a rolling pin into a rough rectangle. Spread the chocolate pastry cream evenly over the dough, then scatter over the chocolate chips. Starting with one of the longer edges, roll the dough up like a Swiss roll. Using a sharp knife, cut the roll into 2cm slices and place the slices, cut side down, on a baking tray. Brush with a little egg wash to glaze and leave to prove for 1¼–1¾ hours until the buns have roughly doubled in size.

Preheat the oven to 220°C/Gas 7. Glaze the buns again and put the tray into the hot oven. Immediately turn the heat down to 180°C/ Gas 4 and bake for 12–15 minutes. As the chocolate dough is quite dark, it can be difficult to tell when the buns are properly cooked – the best way is to lift one gently with a spatula and check that it is firm underneath.

Pain aux raisins and chocolate are two things my son, Jack, loves. He badgered me to make him something that was a cross between the two... the result is pretty gooey, but Jack loves them!

Mary Norwak's
Panettone with Chocolate

MAKES 1 LOAF

125g butter, softened, plus extra
   to grease
25g fresh yeast (or 3 tsp dried
   yeast)
150ml lukewarm water
3 egg yolks, beaten
50g caster sugar
1 tsp salt
1 tsp grated lemon zest

½ tsp vanilla extract
400g strong white bread flour,
   plus extra to dust
100g milk chocolate, chopped
50g sultanas
50g seedless raisins
50g mixed candied peel, chopped
25g butter, melted
icing sugar, to sprinkle

Butter a deep 19–20cm round cake tin. Sprinkle the yeast into the lukewarm water in a small bowl and leave until frothing well.

Put the egg yolks in a large bowl and add the frothy yeast liquid, sugar, salt, lemon zest and vanilla extract. Beat in half of the flour and then gradually beat in the softened butter. Add the remaining flour and knead well for 10 minutes, until the dough is very light and springy. Cover and leave in a warm place to rise for 1 hour.

Turn the dough out onto a lightly floured surface and knead in the chocolate, sultanas, raisins and chopped peel. Form into a ball and put into the prepared cake tin. Cover and leave to prove in a warm place for 45 minutes. Preheat the oven to 200°C/Gas 6.

Brush the risen dough with melted butter and bake in the oven for 20 minutes. Reduce the oven setting to 180°C/Gas 4 and brush the loaf again with melted butter. Bake for a further 30 minutes. Brush with the remaining butter and bake for a final 15 minutes.

Turn the loaf out onto a wire rack to cool. Just before serving, sprinkle thickly with icing sugar.

Favourite Italian cake-bread – usually eaten at Christmas – distinguished by its domed shape and flavouring of sultanas and lemon. It can be made in a Kugelhopf tin, or simply in a deep cake tin.

Elevenses

Everyone needs a little me-time during the day. So why not take a moment, collect your thoughts and replenish the energy levels before throwing yourself back into the day. And with the aroma of fresh coffee in the air, you can put your feet up, breathe and treat yourself to a little something to nibble or even indulge in some naughty dunking.

Choc Nut Biscotti

Australian Women's Weekly

MAKES 60

a little butter, to grease

220g caster sugar

2 eggs

250g plain flour, plus extra
   to dust

1 tsp baking powder

150g shelled pistachio nuts,
   toasted

70g slivered almonds

25g cocoa powder

Preheat the oven to 170°C/Gas 3. Lightly grease a large baking tray. Whisk the sugar and eggs together in a bowl. Sift the flour and baking powder together over the mixture, add the nuts and mix to a sticky dough. Knead the dough on a lightly floured surface, then divide into two portions.

Using floured hands, knead one portion until smooth, but still slightly sticky. Divide this portion into four pieces. Roll each piece into a 25cm log shape. Knead the cocoa powder into the remaining portion until evenly blended, then divide into two pieces. Roll each piece into a 25cm log shape.

Place one chocolate log on the greased baking tray. Place a plain log on each side and press gently together to form a slightly flattened shape. Repeat with the other logs. Bake in the oven for about 30 minutes until lightly browned.

Leave to cool on the tray for 10 minutes. Reduce the oven setting to 140°C/Gas 1. Using a serrated knife, cut the logs diagonally into 5mm thick slices. Place the slices in a single layer on baking trays (ungreased). Bake in the low oven for about 20 minutes or until dry and crisp, turning over halfway through cooking. Transfer to wire racks to cool.

These biscotti can be kept in an airtight container for up to 4 weeks.

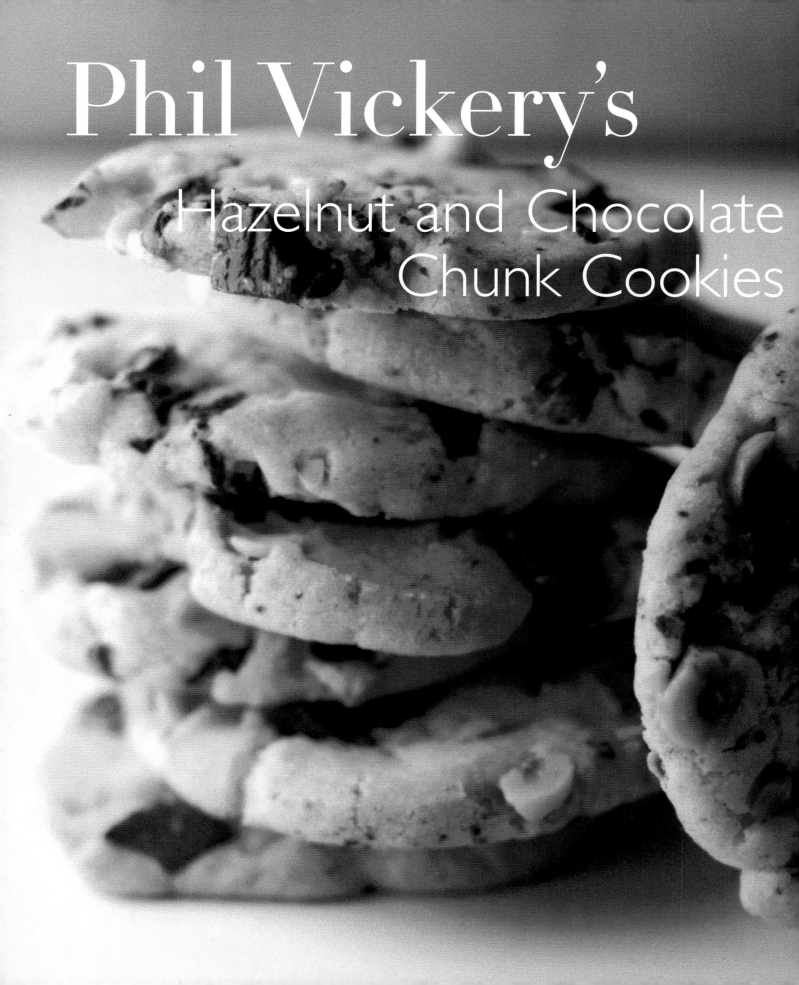

Phil Vickery's

Hazelnut and Chocolate Chunk Cookies

I baked mini versions of these cookies to serve as petits fours when I was head chef at the Castle Hotel in Taunton – they really are that good. Even better, the mixture can be frozen raw, then cut and baked whenever you want fresh cookies.

MAKES ABOUT 30

225g unsalted butter, softened
225g caster sugar
170g sweetened condensed milk

350g self-raising flour, sifted
100g dark chocolate, chopped
100g hazelnuts, roasted and chopped

In a large bowl, cream the butter and sugar together until pale. Stir in the condensed milk, then add the flour and work to a smooth dough. Finally incorporate the chocolate and hazelnuts.

Divide the dough in half and place each portion on a sheet of cling film or foil. Roll each portion into a thick sausage shape and wrap in the film or foil. Chill thoroughly. (This dough will keep quite happily in the fridge for a week or so.)

When ready to bake, preheat the oven to 180°C/Gas 4 and line one or two baking trays with baking parchment. Peel off the cling film or foil, then cut off thick slices of dough (for as many cookies as you need) and place on the baking tray(s). Bake, one tray at a time, for about 15 minutes or until golden brown at the edges, but still a little soft. Transfer to a wire rack to cool.

Constance Spry's
Chocolate Biscuits

MAKES ABOUT 26

225g butter, plus extra to grease
110g caster sugar
1 tsp vanilla extract
50g cocoa powder
225g self-raising flour

FILLING (OPTIONAL):
50g cocoa powder
6 tbsp strong coffee
50g icing sugar, sifted
75–100g butter, diced
few drops of vanilla extract

Preheat the oven to 180°C/Gas 4. Lightly butter one or two baking trays. Cream the butter in a bowl until soft, then beat in the sugar and vanilla extract. Gradually work in the cocoa powder and flour to make a smooth dough.

Divide the mixture into pieces, each the size of a walnut. Roll into balls and place on the baking tray, spacing them apart. Flatten each one with a fork dipped in water, then bake for 12–15 minutes. Leave on the baking tray for a few minutes to firm up, then carefully transfer to a wire rack to cool.

Serve the biscuits just as they are, or fill them if you prefer. To make the filling, heat the cocoa powder with the coffee to make a thick cream, then remove from the heat and gradually beat in the icing sugar, butter to taste, and the vanilla. Leave until cold, then use to sandwich the biscuits together in pairs.

Melt-in-the-mouth chocolate biscuits that can be served plain or sandwiched in pairs with a mocha butter-cream – the more butter, the creamier the filling. Sandwich together just before serving.

Either use fine quality dark chocolate buttons or buy good quality chocolate in a block and chop it coarsely for these biscuits.

Michael Caines'
Chocolate Chip Biscuits

MAKES ABOUT 25
110g unsalted butter
130g caster sugar
60g soft brown sugar
1 tsp vanilla extract
1 egg
110g plain flour

½ tsp baking powder
½ tsp salt
225g dark chocolate, i.e. buttons
  or coarsely chopped
150g chopped walnuts

Cream the butter, sugars and vanilla extract together in a bowl until fluffy. Beat in the egg. Sift the flour with the baking powder and salt and fold into the creamed mixture, followed by the chocolate and walnuts. Cover and chill for 1 hour. Preheat the oven to 160°C/Gas 3.

Roll the mixture into small balls, about the size of a walnut. Place on baking trays, spacing them about 4cm apart. Bake in the oven for about 12 minutes until lightly golden.

Leave on the baking trays for a few minutes to firm up, then transfer to a wire rack to cool. Store in an airtight container.

Mitzie Wilson's
Chocolate Caramel Fingers

MAKES 16
125g butter
50g caster sugar
175g plain flour

CARAMEL FILLING:
125g butter
50g caster sugar
2 tbsp golden syrup
200g sweetened condensed milk

TOPPING:
300g milk chocolate

Preheat the oven to 180°C/Gas 4. Line a shallow 20cm square cake tin with baking parchment.

Beat the butter and sugar together in a bowl until light and creamy. Beat in the flour to form a smooth, soft dough. Spoon the mixture into the prepared tin and press evenly. Bake for 20–25 minutes until pale golden.

Put the filling ingredients in a saucepan over a low heat. Stir to dissolve the sugar, then turn up the heat and allow to boil for about 5–7 minutes, stirring all the time. The mixture is ready when it turns a deep golden caramel colour and has thickened to a soft fudgey consistency. Pour over the shortbread and leave to set for an hour or so, until chewy.

Turn the caramel-topped shortbread out onto a surface lined with baking parchment and then turn the right way up. Peel off the paper and cut into fingers using a hot, wet knife. Place the fingers on a wire cooling rack over a plate. (If the caramel is still a little soft and difficult to cut, don't worry it can be cut after topping with chocolate once it has set.)

For the topping, melt the milk chocolate (see page 13). Pour a spoonful of melted chocolate along the top of each finger and spread with a small palette knife to coat the top and sides. Allow to set in a cool place. Store in an airtight tin for up to 1 week.

Buttery shortbread fingers, topped with fudgey caramel and coated in milk chocolate... simply divine!

Popular with kids, these small crispies need to be kept somewhere cool in warm weather. If you haven't any paper cases, spoon the mixture directly onto a tray lined with baking parchment in small mounds. For a more generous size, you could make about 12.

Mary Berry's
Chocolate Crispies

MAKES 18
225g dark chocolate, in pieces
1 tbsp golden syrup
50g butter
75g cornflakes

Set 18 paper cake cases on a large baking tray.

Put the chocolate, golden syrup and butter in a heavy-based pan over a low heat and allow to melt, stirring occasionally. Take off the heat and add the cornflakes, stirring gently until they are all evenly coated in the chocolate mixture.

Divide the mixture evenly between the paper cases and place in the fridge until set.

No-bake Chocolate Slice

Australian Women's Weekly

24 SLICES

90g butter, in pieces, plus extra
  to grease
200g white marshmallows
1 tbsp water
200g dark chocolate, coarsely
  chopped
125g digestives or rich tea biscuits,
  coarsely chopped

125g glacé cherries, halved
75g roasted hazelnuts, halved
50g walnut halves, broken
  into pieces

TOPPING:
200g dark chocolate
60g butter

Grease two shallow 8cm x 25cm oblong baking tins (or plastic containers with similar dimensions). Line the bases and sides with baking parchment, allowing the paper to extend 2cm above the long edges.

Put the marshmallows, water and butter into a medium saucepan and stir constantly over a low heat until the marshmallows have melted and the mixture is smooth. Remove the pan from the heat. Add the chocolate and stir until melted. Add the biscuits, cherries and nuts, and stir gently until evenly combined.

Divide the mixture between the baking tins and spread evenly (do not crush the biscuits). Cover and chill for 1 hour.

For the topping, melt the chocolate and butter together in a pan over simmering water. Stir until smooth and let cool slightly. Spread the mixture evenly over the no-bake slices and chill for 1 hour or until firm.

Lift the chocolate slices out of the tins, using the paper, then peel off the lining paper. Cut each slice into 12 pieces.

This more-ish slice can be kept in an airtight container in the fridge for up to a week. Try using pecans in place of the walnuts.

Chocolate Panforte
Australian Women's Weekly

SERVES 30

a little butter, to grease
2 sheets of rice paper
110g plain flour
2 tbsp cocoa powder
¼ tsp ground cinnamon
¼ tsp ground ginger
150g glacé figs, coarsely chopped
125g glacé peaches or pineapple, coarsely chopped
100g glacé cherries (ideally ½ red, ½ green, halved

85g dates, pitted and halved
80g blanched almonds, toasted
75g unsalted cashew nuts, toasted
75g hazelnuts, toasted
75g macadamia nuts, toasted
120g honey
75g caster sugar
75g brown sugar
2 tbsp water
100g dark chocolate

Make this panforte a day in advance to allow time for the flavours to develop. You will need to line the tin with rice paper. Contrary to popular belief, this edible paper is not actually made from rice, but from the pith of a small tree that grows in Asia. Rice paper can be found in specialist food stores and delicatessens.

Preheat the oven to 150°C/Gas 2. Grease a 20cm sandwich tin and line the base with rice paper, cutting the sheets to fit. Sift the flour, cocoa powder and spices together into a large bowl and stir in the fruit and nuts.

Combine the honey, sugars and water in a small saucepan and stir over a low heat until the sugar dissolves, then simmer, without stirring, for 5 minutes.

Meanwhile, melt the chocolate (see page 13).

Pour the hot syrup onto the fruit and nut mixture, followed by the chocolate. Stir until well combined. Press the mixture firmly into the prepared tin and bake in the oven for about 45 minutes.

Leave to cool in the tin, then remove and wrap in foil. Leave to stand overnight. Cut the panforte into thin wedges to serve.

Served warm with a rich, creamy, chocolate sauce these make a great pudding, or you can serve them without the sauce for elevenses.

Chocolate Polenta Cakes
Australian Women's Weekly

MAKES 8

125g butter, softened, plus extra
   to grease
150g caster sugar
150g ground almonds
25g cocoa powder, sifted
50g dark chocolate, grated
2 eggs

85g instant polenta
80ml milk

CHOCOLATE SAUCE (OPTIONAL):
125ml double cream
125g dark chocolate, in pieces

Preheat the oven to 170°C/Gas 3. Grease 8 individual oval tins or muffin tins (80ml capacity). Line the bases with baking parchment.

Beat the butter and sugar together using a hand-held electric beater until light and fluffy. Add the ground almonds, cocoa powder and chocolate, and mix until just combined. Add the eggs, one at a time, beating well between each addition. Combine the polenta with the milk and stir into the mixture.

Divide the mixture between the prepared tins. Bake in the oven for 25–30 minutes until cooked. Turn out onto a wire rack, remove the paper and leave to cool slightly.

To make the chocolate sauce if serving, combine the chocolate and cream in a heatproof bowl and stir over a pan of simmering water until melted. Serve the cakes warm, with or without the warm chocolate sauce poured over.

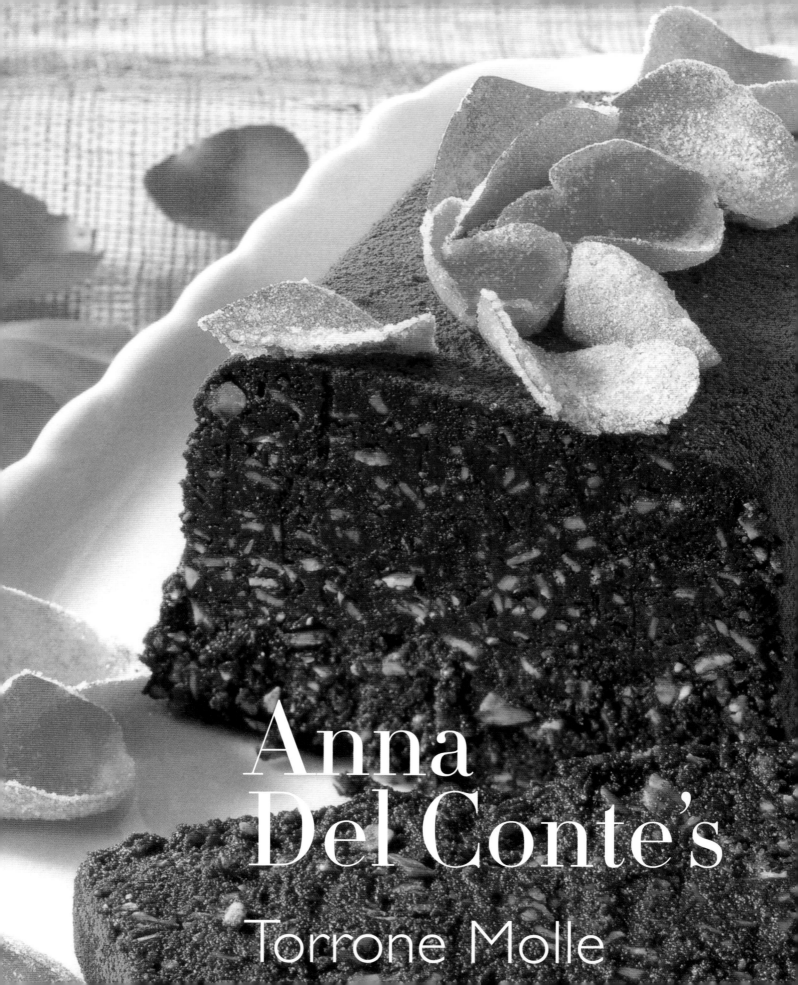

Anna
Del Conte's
Torrone Molle

Torrone is a traditional

confection in northern Italy and this particular recipe is from my family home. It is usually served as a pudding, though it is delicious with coffee at any time of the day. Use fine quality cocoa powder and freshly blanched, skinned almonds.

SERVES 8

115g almonds in their skins, blanched and peeled
200g unsalted butter
200g granulated sugar
115g cocoa powder
1 large egg, plus 1 large egg yolk

115g digestives or other plain biscuits
2 tbsp dark rum
crystallised flowers, such as violets or rose petals, and/or blanched or sugared almonds, to decorate

Preheat the oven to 180°C/ Gas 4. Line a 600ml loaf tin with cling film. Spread the blanched almonds on a baking tray and bake for 7–10 minutes until they turn golden. Cool slightly, then whiz in a food processor until very coarsely ground.

Cream the butter and sugar together until light and fluffy. Add the cocoa powder, a spoonful at a time, and beat hard until completely incorporated. (This can be done in a food processor.) Now mix in the freshly ground almonds. Lightly beat the whole egg and egg yolk together, then add to the mixture, stirring until well blended.

Crush the biscuits with a rolling pin and add to the mix with the rum. Mix thoroughly, then spoon the mixture into the prepared tin. Press down well and level the top with a spatula. Cover with cling film and refrigerate for at least 4 hours.

Decorate with crystallised flowers and/or blanched or sugared almonds to serve.

Jill Norman's
Chocolate Walnut Torte

SERVES 8–10

butter, to grease
120g walnut halves
60g ready-to-eat pitted dates
60g ready-to-eat dried apricots
60g glacé cherries or pineapple
60g crystallised citron or orange
   peel

3 tbsp plain flour, plus extra
   to dust
1 tsp baking powder
¼ tsp ground cinnamon
2 eggs
180g caster sugar
60g dark chocolate, grated

Preheat the oven to 150°C/Gas 2. Butter and flour a 22cm round
cake tin. Chop the nuts, fruit and peel by hand, rather than in a
processor (which can produce a pulp rather than pieces) and place
in a bowl. Sift together the flour, baking powder and cinnamon.

Beat the eggs until pale and fluffy, then beat in the sugar and the
flour mixture. Add the nut and fruit mix, along with the chocolate.
Mix well and pour into the prepared tin. Smooth the surface and
bake in the oven for 45–50 minutes until the torte is golden brown.

Transfer to a rack to cool, then wrap and chill overnight if
possible. Serve with whipped cream, if you like.

This rich torte always seems
to meet with approval. As the texture is
quite soft and sticky, it's best made a day
before it is eaten, to allow it to firm up.

Use bitter chocolate – high in cocoa solids – rather than a medium dark chocolate for these brownies, to avoid an overly sweet aftertaste.

Jeremy Lee's
Chocolate Brownies

MAKES 15

225g unsalted butter
115g dark bitter chocolate
4 large eggs
375g caster sugar

50g plain flour
50g cocoa powder
½ tsp vanilla extract
75g chopped walnuts (optional)

Preheat the oven to 200°C/Gas 6. Line a 25cm round or square cake tin with baking parchment. Put the butter and chocolate in a bowl over a pan of simmering water to melt – don't stir or touch the contents during melt-down.

In a large bowl, whisk the eggs and sugar together until they treble in volume. Sift the flour with the cocoa powder over the mixture and add the vanilla extract, the melted chocolate mixture and walnuts, if using. Mix the whole lot together. Pour the batter into the prepared tin and bake for about 40 minutes (the less the brownie is cooked, the better, so err to less.)

Allow the brownies to cool completely before cutting. Store in an airtight container in a cool, dark place … if they get that far.

Mrs Asbeck's Stollen
Jane Suthering

SERVES 10–12

55g fresh yeast, or 30g dried yeast
250ml lukewarm water
115g caster sugar, plus an extra
   1 tbsp to dust
500g strong white bread flour,
  plus extra to dust
¾ tsp salt
¼ tsp ground cardamom
¼ tsp freshly grated nutmeg
¼ tsp ground cinnamon
255g unsalted butter, diced and
   softened, plus extra to grease
finely grated zest of ½ lemon

85g currants
225g sultanas
85g candied orange peel, diced
85g candied lemon peel, diced
85g flaked almonds
1 tbsp icing sugar, to dust

CHOCOLATE MARZIPAN:
115g dark chocolate
115g ground almonds
30g caster sugar
1 egg white

Dissolve the yeast in the lukewarm water and add 1 tbsp of the caster sugar. Sift the flour, salt and spices into a bowl and make a well in the centre. Pour in the yeast mixture and leave in a warm place for about 20 minutes, until the yeast liquid is frothy.

Add the remaining sugar, 225g of the butter and the grated lemon zest and beat to a soft dough. Using an electric mixer fitted with a dough hook if possible, knead well for about 10 minutes. Cover the bowl with a tea-towel and leave to rise in a warm place for 30–45 minutes, until doubled in size.

Knead the dough again for about 5 minutes, then work in the fruit and nuts. Cover and leave to rise again in a warm place for 30–45 minutes, until doubled in size.

Meanwhile, make the marzipan. Melt the chocolate (see page 13) and cool slightly. Combine the ground almonds, sugar and egg white in a bowl. Add the chocolate and mix to a smooth paste.

On a lightly floured surface, knead the dough quickly, then press it out roughly to an oval shape about 40cm long. Roll the marzipan into a cylinder, about 2cm thick and 30cm long. Place in the centre of the dough, then fold both long edges in over the marzipan and tuck the shorter ends under to enclose the marzipan completely.

Set the dough on a lightly buttered large baking tray. Cover and leave in a warm place for about 1 hour until well risen – the dough should spring back when lightly pressed with the fingertips. Preheat the oven to 200°C/Gas 6.

Christmas wouldn't be the same without this festive treat. Mrs Asbeck, the mother of my closest friend from school, made one of the best stollens I've ever tasted and kindly gave me her recipe. I've reproduced it here, adding a chocolate marzipan centre to make it even more tempting... if that's possible!

Bake the stollen in the oven for 30 minutes. Lower the oven setting to 180°C/Gas 4 and bake for a further 15–20 minutes until golden brown and cooked through. To test, tap the base of the stollen with your knuckles – it should sound hollow. If it appears to be browning too quickly before it is cooked, cover loosely with foil.

Melt the remaining 30g butter and brush over the stollen while it is still warm. Sprinkle with 1 tbsp caster sugar, then sift the icing sugar over the top. Allow to cool on a wire rack.

Serve cut into slices. If the stollen ever gets the chance to become dry, it is also delicious toasted!

A luxurious bread that is unlikely to give you any leftovers, but if it does, use them to make an extra-rich bread and butter pudding.

Paul Hollywood's
Chocolate and Cherry Bread

MAKES 2 LOAVES

500g strong white bread flour, plus extra to dust

15g fresh yeast

2 tsp salt

1 tbsp caster sugar

30ml olive oil

about 250ml warm water to mix

160g well-drained canned black cherries

200g plain chocolate, chopped, or chocolate chips

Put the flour into a bowl and rub in the yeast using your fingertips. Stir in the salt, sugar and olive oil, then slowly add enough warm water to make a pliable dough, mixing by hand. Tip the dough onto a lightly floured surface and knead for 4–7 minutes until smooth. Place in a clean bowl, cover with a tea-towel and leave to rise in a warm place for 1 hour. Line a baking tray with baking parchment.

Divide the dough into two pieces and knead half of the cherries into each portion, adding a little more flour if the dough becomes too wet. Now knead half the chocolate into each portion, again, adding a little flour if necessary.

Shape each portion into a ball and flatten to a 5cm depth. Dust heavily with flour and score diagonal lines across the top to form a diamond pattern. Place on the baking tray, cover loosely and leave to prove for 1 hour. Preheat the oven to 200°C/Gas 6.

Bake the bread for 20–25 minutes until it sounds hollow when tapped on the underside with your knuckles. Transfer to a wire rack to cool.

Glynn Christian's
Chocolate Cardamom Loaf

10 SLICES

225g butter, plus extra to grease
100g dark chocolate (70% cocoa
  solids)
75g seedless raisins (ideally
  Muscatels)
225g golden caster sugar

4 small eggs
400g self-raising flour, sifted
seeds from 10 cardamom pods,
  finely crushed
200ml full-fat milk

Preheat the oven to 190°C/Gas 5. Butter a 1kg loaf tin and line the base with greaseproof paper. Roughly cut up the chocolate so the pieces are about the same size as your seedless raisins.

Cream the butter and sugar together in a bowl until smooth and light, then beat in the eggs one at a time. Toss the flour and cardamom together and stir into the mixture, alternating with the milk until evenly combined; don't over-beat. The mixture should have a soft dropping consistency. Fold in the chocolate and raisins.

Spoon the mixture into the prepared loaf tin and bake for 1 hour – 1 hour 10 minutes, covering loosely with greaseproof paper towards the end if it appears to be browning too quickly. Leave in the tin for 10 minutes, then turn out onto a wire rack to cool before slicing.

Cardamom is the perfect spice to complement the piquancy of chocolate. The fun of this loaf is that you never quite know what the next bite will be – sweet fruity raisins or voluptuous chocolate.

À La Carte

Don't think for a moment that you have to deprive yourself of chocolate's sensuous charms when your mind turns to savoury dishes. After all, thanks to the ancient civilisations of South America, cocoa has been used this way for over 3,500 years. So dive in and discover what chocolate's melt-in-the-mouth qualities can do for lunch and dinner.

Lynda Brown's
Chocolate Pasta

MAKES 500G

3 eggs
about 300g '00' pasta flour,
    plus extra to dust
30g cocoa powder

RICOTTA AND BRANDY SAUCE
(OPTIONAL):
225g ricotta cheese, sieved
1–2 tbsp brandy
about 4 tbsp creamy milk or
    single cream
2 tbsp flaked almonds or pine
    nuts, toasted, to serve

Break the eggs into a food processor and process briefly for about 15 seconds to mix. Sift 275g of the flour and the cocoa powder together and tip into the food processor. Process for 30–60 seconds until the dough comes away from the sides of the bowl and forms a ball. The precise amount of flour needed will depend on the size of the eggs and the absorbency of the flour you use.

Knead the dough briefly on a floured surface. If it still feels sticky, work in a little more sifted flour as you knead. The finished dough should be neither too firm or too soft; it should feel smooth, elastic and malleable, but not sticky. It is now ready to use; or you can wrap it in a plastic bag and keep it in the fridge for later; or freeze it.

Roll out the dough thinly using a pasta machine if you have one. Otherwise, knead the dough briefly on a lightly floured surface and divide into 4 portions. Roll out one quarter at a time to a long strip, about 1–2mm thick. Cut into long, thin strips, about 1cm wide, using a pasta machine or by hand. Make sure the strips don't touch each other and leave them to rest for 30 minutes, or until you want to cook the pasta. Repeat with the rest of the dough.

To make the sauce if serving, mix the ricotta with the brandy and enough milk or cream to make a smooth sauce, the consistency of double cream.

To cook the pasta, have a large pan of boiling salted water ready. Throw in the pasta, swirl around and cook for 1–3 minutes, until *al dente* – cooked, but with some bite. The timing depends on how much the pasta has dried out before you cook it. Test a strand after 1 minute, and frequently until cooked. Drain as soon as it is ready.

Either toss the pasta in a little butter or cream if eating plain, or with the ricotta and brandy sauce, or other sauce of your choice. Sprinkle with toasted nuts if you like and serve immediately.

This quantity of pasta is enough to serve 4–6 as a starter, 3–4 as a main course, or up to 6 as a dessert. I always use organic ingredients.

Chocolate pasta ... Why not? The taste is not nearly as odd or you'd imagine, and the colour – a deep, rich, chocolate brown – is magnificent. It's perfect with strong flavoured game such as pigeon, hare, venison and wild duck; or try serving it as a dessert with chestnut honey, cream, a little finely grated seriously dark chocolate and a pinch of ground cinnamon.

Aiden Byrne's
White Chocolate and Truffle Risotto

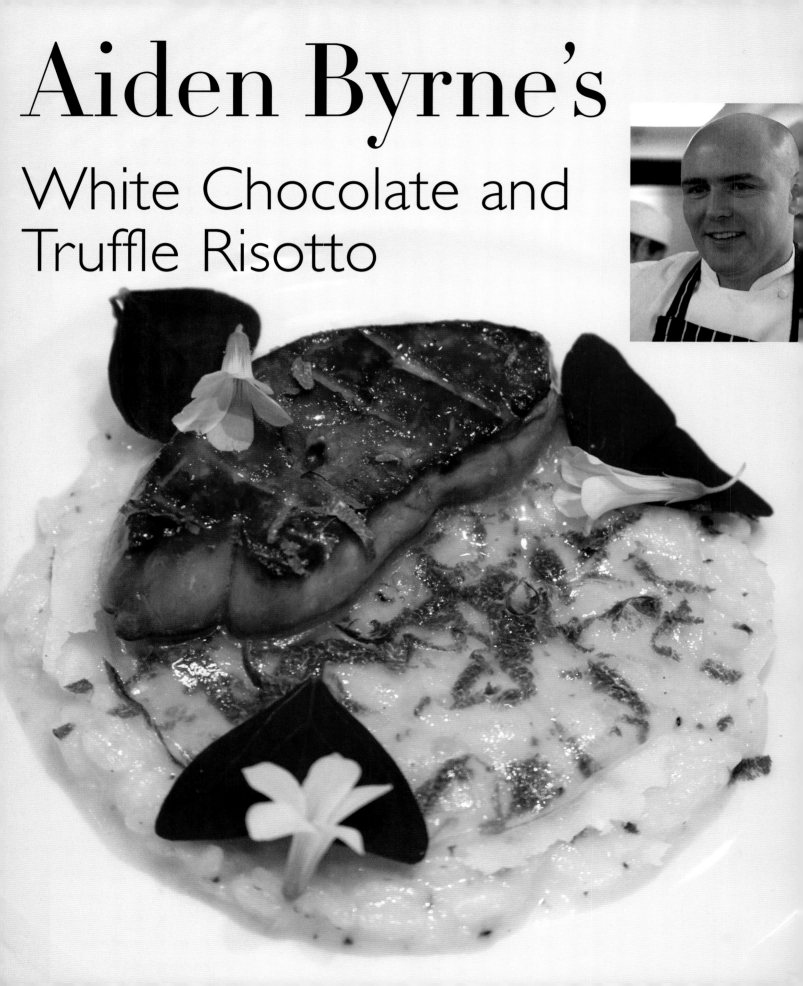

White chocolate in a savoury risotto may seem unusual, but this sophisticated, original recipe is amazing. Use a good light chicken stock and infuse it with the truffle trimmings – it will make all the difference to the flavour. I garnish with oxalis leaves and flowers; wood sorrel is a good alternative.

SERVES 4
50g fresh truffle
50g unsalted butter
3 banana shallots, finely chopped
125g risotto rice (e.g. Carnaroli)
150ml white wine
1.5 litres hot, light chicken stock (infused with truffle trimmings)
2 tbsp truffle oil
75g mascarpone
30g Parmesan, half of it grated
juice of 1 lemon, or to taste
25g white chocolate, finely chopped

BANANA JELLY:
4 large bananas, chopped
300ml sugar syrup (see page 15)
2 sheets of leaf gelatine
½ tsp powdered agar agar
sunflower oil, for brushing

SMOKED FOIE GRAS:
300g foie gras (premium grade)
salt
100g wood shavings
1 tbsp sherry vinegar

Chop three-quarters of the truffle. Melt the butter in a pan, add the shallots and two-thirds of the chopped truffle, cover and sweat gently without colouring for 2–3 minutes. Add the rice, stir and cook for 1 minute, again without colouring.

Add the wine, turn the heat up slightly and stir until absorbed. Add the stock 100ml at a time, stirring. Ensure each addition is absorbed before adding the next. When you've added three-quarters of it, take a small spoonful of rice to see if it is ready. (The rice should be slightly undercooked, so you can reheat it later). Add a little more stock and continue cooking for a bit longer if necessary. When the risotto is at the right stage, tip it onto a large tray and spread it out evenly. Cover with greaseproof paper to stop the rice drying out and leave to cool. Once cold, store in the fridge.

For the banana jelly, warm the sugar syrup, take off the heat, add the bananas and leave to infuse for 4 hours. Soften the gelatine in cold water. Strain half the infused syrup into a pan, add the agar-agar and bring to the boil. Pass the rest of the syrup through a fine sieve into a bowl. Squeeze the gelatine to remove excess water and add to the hot syrup, stirring to dissolve, then stir in the cold syrup. Pass through a sieve again. Line four dinner plates with cling film, oil lightly and pour a quarter of the syrup onto each plate. Chill to set.

Dip a long, thin knife into hot water and slice the foie gras into 4 even slices. Lay on a wire rack and place in the freezer for a couple of hours (to prevent it from melting when you smoke it later).

Heat your oven as high as it will go, open the kitchen windows and door and turn your extractor fan on full blast. Heat a sturdy baking tray in the bottom of the oven for 30 minutes. Season the frozen foie gras with salt. Open the oven door and sprinkle the wood chippings liberally across the baking tray. Close the door for 20 seconds to allow the smoke to build up, then standing well back, open the oven door and set the wire rack of foie gras over the wood chippings. Close the door immediately and leave for 1½ minutes. With a folded oven cloth, remove the tray of chippings and the foie gras. Take the chippings outside and let them burn away on the tray. Put the smoked foie gras in the fridge to stop it cooking.

Heat 100ml of the remaining stock in a wide pan, then add the cooked rice and stir gently with a wooden spoon. Add the remaining chopped truffle and truffle oil, then the mascarpone, grated Parmesan, lemon juice and finally the chocolate. Taste and adjust the seasoning. You might like to add a little more mascarpone for extra creaminess, lemon juice for freshness or white chocolate for sweetness (allowing for the sweetness of the banana jelly and the saltiness of the Parmesan).

Heat a non-stick frying pan, add the smoked foie gras and sear quickly on all sides until it is soft in the centre, then drizzle over the sherry vinegar. Spoon the risotto onto warm plates. Shave the rest of the truffle and Parmesan over. Peel the banana jelly sheets off the cling film and lay one on each portion. Top with the foie gras.

McRae's
Sautéed Tiger Prawns
with chocolate sauce

SERVES 4

125ml extra-virgin olive oil
2 onions, finely chopped
1 bay leaf
1 tsp finely chopped thyme, plus
 sprigs to garnish
1 small ham bone (optional)
1kg firm, ripe tomatoes, diced
1 litre water

16 large tiger prawns, each
 about 50–60g, cleaned
salt and black pepper
3 garlic cloves, finely chopped
50g blanched almonds, toasted
 and finely chopped
125g dark chocolate, melted
 (see page 13)

Heat 2 tbsp of the olive oil in a saucepan over a medium heat and sauté the onions with the bay leaf, thyme, and ham bone if using, for 8–10 minutes or until lightly browned. Stir in the tomatoes. Lower the heat, cover and cook for 15 minutes. Pour in the water and let bubble to reduce by half. Strain the sauce.

Season the prawns with salt and pepper. Heat the remaining oil in a large frying pan over a medium heat and fry the prawns for about 3–5 minutes or until pink. Remove from the pan with a slotted spoon, saving the oil in the pan, and arrange the prawns on serving plates.

Drizzle the strained sauce over the prawns. Mix the garlic, almonds and chocolate together in a small bowl. Stir in 4 tbsp of the reserved oil, then spoon over the prawns and serve, garnished with thyme.

This Catalan dish is traditionally made with langoustines or Dublin Bay prawns, so use these if you like – to give the dish authenticity.

Jenny Chandler's
Rich Chocolate Picada

SERVES 4–6

2 tbsp olive oil
1 slice of white bread
25g dark, bittersweet chocolate
3 garlic cloves, peeled but left whole
salt and black pepper

½ tsp ground cinnamon
6 roasted almonds
6 roasted hazelnuts
2 tbsp chopped flat-leaf parsley
extra virgin olive oil, to bind

A picada is a Spanish ground blend of herbs, nuts, garlic, spices, bread and, in this case, chocolate, which is added to a dish a few minutes before serving – to season, enrich and thicken the sauce. The ingredients are traditionally pounded together with a large pestle and mortar, but you could use a small blender or food processor instead. This picada is particularly suited to game and red meat dishes.

Heat the olive oil in a frying pan. Add the bread and fry until crisp and golden, then remove and chop into small pieces. Finely chop or grate the chocolate.

Pound the garlic with a good pinch of salt in a large mortar with a pestle, then add the chocolate, cinnamon, nuts and parsley. Keep grinding until you have a paste, then add the bread and just enough olive oil to bind everything together.

Once the picada is thoroughly mixed and smooth it is ready to use.

Joanna Farrow's
Sweet and Sour Chicken

SERVES 4

4 chicken supremes, or breast fillets, skinned
salt and black pepper
50g butter
1 fennel bulb, finely chopped
75g sliced pancetta, cut into thin strips
2 garlic cloves, crushed
2 bay leaves
4 tbsp red wine vinegar
1 tbsp dark muscovado sugar
200ml rich chicken or game stock
50g sultanas
25g dark, bitter chocolate (85% cocoa solids), chopped
25g pine nuts, toasted

Score each chicken breast several times on the skinned side and season with salt and pepper.

Melt half the butter in a large frying pan and gently fry the fennel for 5 minutes until softened. Add the pancetta and garlic and fry for 2–3 minutes until the pancetta starts to brown and crisp. Push the ingredients to one side of the pan.

Add the remaining butter to the pan. When melted, add the chicken, scored side down, and fry briefly until browned. Turn the pieces and brown on the underside.

Add the bay leaves, wine vinegar, sugar and stock and heat until bubbling. Reduce the heat to low and cook for 20–25 minutes or until the chicken is tender. Remove the chicken and keep warm.

Add the sultanas and chocolate to the pan and cook very gently, stirring for 2–3 minutes. Season the sauce with salt and pepper to taste. Return the chicken to the pan and spoon over the sauce. Scatter with pine nuts and serve.

Dark, bitter chocolate adds a rich flavour and velvety texture to the tangy sauce for this simple chicken dish without overpowering it. Serve on a bed of creamy mash or polenta to soak up the juices.

Elisabeth Luard's
Turkey in Chilli Sauce
with chocolate

Put the turkey crown in a pan with the onion, cloves, allspice, peppercorns, herbs and a little salt. Pour in enough water to cover and bring to a simmer. Poach gently for 1½–2 hours, until perfectly tender – the liquid should tremble rather than bubble. Lift out the turkey, strip the meat from the bones and set aside. Strain the broth and reserve.

To make the sauce, toast the chillies in a dry frying pan for about 1 minute until they change colour, then tip them into a small bowl and pour on enough boiling water to cover.

Heat half the fat in the frying pan and fry the tortilla pieces until crisp and brown, then tip into a blender. Toss the nuts and pumpkin seeds in the fat left in the pan and stir over the heat to toast a little, then add to the blender. Add the tomatoes to the pan with a little more fat if needed and fry until soft and soupy. Stir in the raisins and let bubble briefly, then add to the blender. Add about 300ml of the reserved broth, and process to a thick purée.

Heat the remaining fat in the pan and fry the garlic and onion until soft and golden. Add the contents of the blender and bubble up, then lower the heat and leave to simmer gently for 15 minutes.

Meanwhile, tip the soaked chillies and their water into the blender and whiz until evenly blended. Stir the chilli paste into the sauce in the pan (adding as much as your taste buds can cope with!) and bubble up. Stir in the chocolate, orange zest and cinnamon. Add another 600ml of the reserved broth and bubble up again. Add the turkey meat and simmer for 20 minutes until the oily sauce begins to pool a little. Season with salt to taste.

Heap the turkey mole onto a warm serving dish and scatter with extra pumpkin seeds and a few orange zest strips. Serve with black beans, white rice, guacamole and soft tortillas for scooping.

SERVES 10–12
1 turkey crown (from a medium
  turkey)
1 large onion, cut into chunks
3 cloves
3 allspice berries
6 peppercorns
2–3 thyme sprigs
2–3 sprigs or 1 tsp dried
  marjoram or oregano
salt

SAUCE:
125g dried medium-hot chillies,
  deseeded and torn
6 tbsp rendered pork fat or oil
1 maize flour tortilla, torn into
  small pieces
4 tbsp roughly chopped peanuts
2 tbsp pumpkin seeds, plus extra
  to finish
2–3 tomatilloes (or ordinary
  tomatoes), chopped
4 tbsp raisins
6 garlic cloves, roughly chopped
1 onion, finely sliced
50g dark chocolate, grated
1 tsp finely grated orange zest,
  plus a few strips to finish
1 tsp ground cinnamon
salt

Turkey mole as this is commonly known is one of the great dishes of the Mexican kitchen. It is said to have been invented by the nuns of a convent in Oaxaca. Don't be intimidated by the length of the ingredient list – the cooking is easy.

Matthew Fort's
Pan-fried Pigeon
with black and white pudding

SERVES 4

a little vegetable oil
50g butter
8 pigeon breasts, skinned
4 slices of black pudding
4 slices of white pudding
salt and black pepper

dash of brandy
splash of creamy stout
500ml chicken stock
100g dark chocolate, chopped
2 oranges, segmented
bunch of watercress, trimmed

Heat a little oil in a frying pan, add the butter and fry the pigeon breasts for a couple of minutes on each side, then remove to an ovenproof plate. Add the black and white pudding to the pan and fry for 2½ minutes on each side, then season with salt and pepper. Add to the pigeon and keep warm in a low oven.

Add the brandy and stout to the pan, scraping up the sediment to deglaze. Let bubble, then stir in the stock and bring to the boil. Turn the heat down to a simmer, add the chocolate, stirring until melted.

Divide the slices of black and white pudding between 4 plates, top with the pigeon breasts and drizzle over the sauce. Toss the orange segments with the watercress and serve on the side.

Succulent pigeon breasts are pan-fried with black and white pudding, then served with a tangy orange and watercress salad to cut the richness.

Joanna Farrow's
Calves' Liver
with chocolate balsamic glaze

SERVES 4

750g sweet potatoes	600g thinly sliced calves liver
250g floury potatoes	8 rashers dry-cured back bacon
salt and black pepper	1 tbsp olive oil
75g butter	3 tbsp balsamic vinegar
2 tsp finely chopped thyme, plus	1 tbsp water
extra to garnish	15g dark, bitter chocolate, chopped

Cut all the potatoes into chunks. Cook in boiling salted water for 20 minutes or until tender. Drain, return to the pan and mash with 50g butter, the thyme and plenty of pepper. Cover and keep warm.

Season the liver on both sides. Heat a large frying pan and fry the bacon until crisp. Remove and keep warm. Melt the remaining butter in the pan with the olive oil and fry the liver for 1–2 minutes on each side until golden and tender. Remove to a warm plate. Add the balsamic vinegar and 1 tbsp water to the pan and let it bubble up. Take off the heat and stir in the chocolate until melted.

Spoon the mash onto serving plates and top with the liver and bacon. Drizzle with the glaze and serve scattered with thyme.

Creamy calves' liver, salty bacon and a tangy chocolate balsamic glaze make a great partnership in this simple supper. Prepare the mash first and keep it warm as the liver cooks in minutes.

Lindsey Bareham's
Duck with Salsa Agrodolce

SERVES 2
500ml chicken stock
4 garlic cloves, smashed
2 skinless duck breast fillets

ONION MARMALADE:
2 tbsp olive oil
2 large onions, sliced
salt and black pepper

½ tsp dried chilli flakes
1 tbsp dark brown sugar
2 tbsp red wine vinegar
1 small glass red wine (about 150ml)
25g dark chocolate (about 70% cocoa solids), chopped

First make the onion marmalade. Heat the olive oil in a large frying pan or wok over a medium heat. Add the onions and cook, stirring frequently, until they begin to wilt and take on some colour. Reduce the heat after 5–6 minutes, season the onions with ½ tsp salt and cook for a further 10 minutes, possibly longer, until floppy and juicy. Stir in the chilli flakes and then the sugar. Season with pepper and cook until the onions are sticky, slippery and dark. Don't hurry this – the onions must be really tender and caramelised.

Transfer the mixture to a medium heavy-based pan and add the wine vinegar and wine. Bring to the boil, stirring a couple of times, then reduce the heat so it simmers very, very gently. Partially cover and leave to cook for at least an hour. The result you're after is thick, juicy and jam-like. Add the chocolate, stirring until melted. Use immediately or leave to cool slightly, then decant into a jar, cover, cool and refrigerate.

To cook the duck, pour the stock into a pan (that can accommodate the fillets submerged). Add the garlic and simmer for 15 minutes. Immerse the duck fillets in the stock and simmer very gently for 10 minutes. Turn off the heat and leave for 5 minutes.

Meanwhile, for the salsa agrodolce, strain 100ml of the stock into another pan, add 2 tbsp onion marmalade or more to taste, and heat, stirring, until evenly blended.

Slice the duck breasts thickly, divide between two warmed plates and spoon over the salsa agrodolce to serve. Ideal accompaniments are peas or green beans, and either diced potatoes fried in duck fat or mashed potato.

Duck breasts are poached in a garlic-infused stock and served with a sweet-sour sauce flavoured with onion marmalade. The marmalade has a gentle chilli kick and the chocolate gives it a luscious creamy texture. It will keep in the fridge for several weeks, but I find it doesn't last long. It's delicious with cheese, pâté and char-grilled liver, and as a bruschetta base.

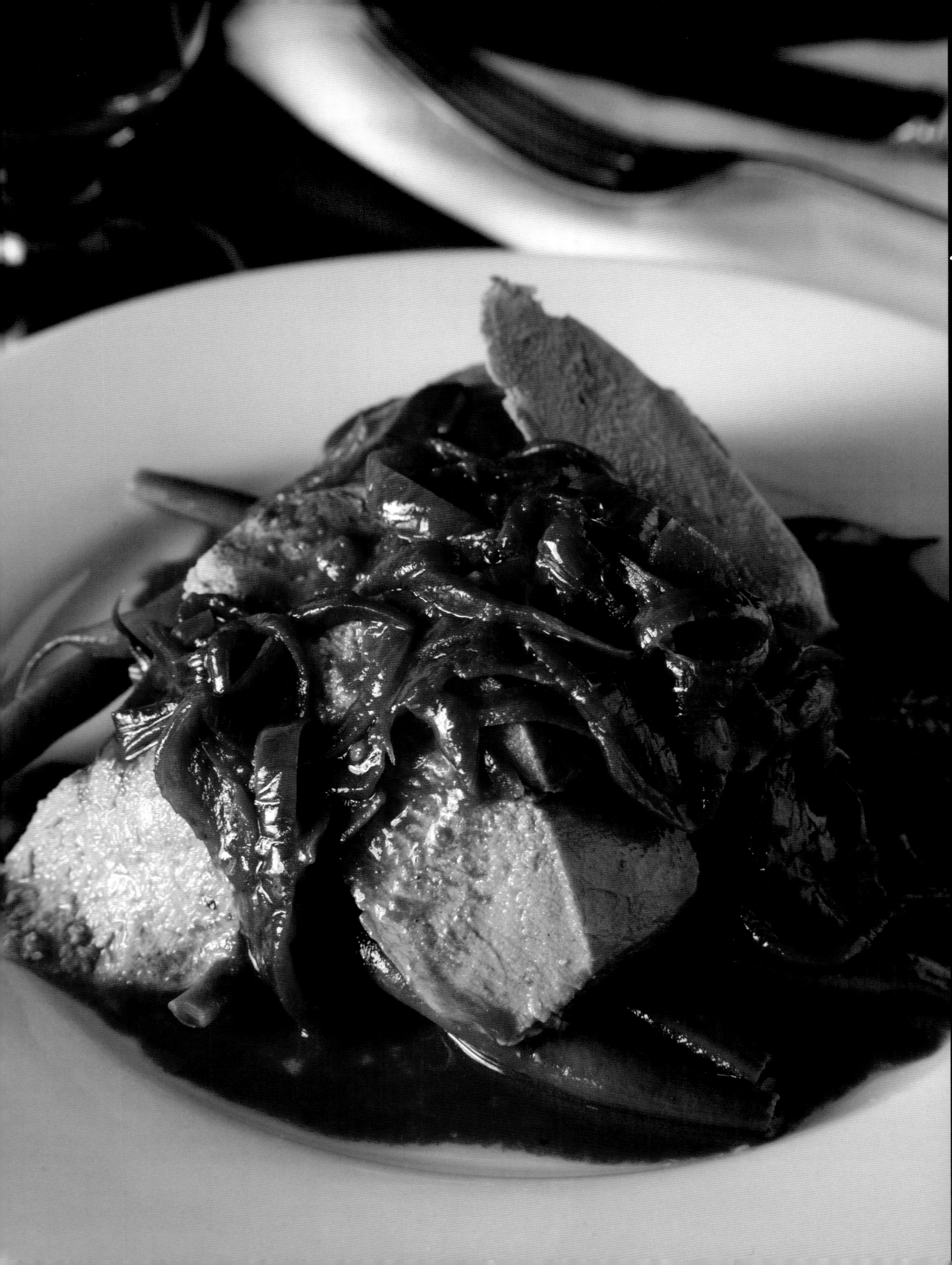

Hotel Chocolat 101 Best Loved Chocolate Recipes

Carol Wilson's
Chilli con Carne

SERVES 4

2 tbsp oil
2 onions, chopped
450g lean minced beef
1 tsp dried oregano
1 tsp ground cinnamon
1 small green chilli
1 tbsp molasses sugar

400g can tomatoes
400g can red kidney beans
55g dark chocolate, in pieces
salt
coriander or flat-leaf parsley
   sprigs, to garnish

Heat the oil in a large heavy-based pan. Add the chopped onions and cook over a medium heat for 5 minutes or so until soft. Increase the heat, add the minced beef and cook, stirring, for a few minutes until evenly browned. Reduce the heat and add the oregano and cinnamon.

Cut open the chilli and scrape out the seeds under running water, then chop finely. Add to the pan with the molasses sugar, tomatoes and kidney beans. Stir in the chocolate and season well with salt. Cover and simmer gently for 1 hour, stirring from time to time to prevent sticking and adding a little water if necessary.

Serve garnished with coriander or parsley, and accompanied by boiled rice or crusty bread and a green salad.

This chilli is mild – if you prefer to make it hotter, increase the chillies to two or three. The molasses sugar and chocolate darken the sauce and add a deep richness to the flavour of the dish.

Prue Leith's

Slow Roast Lamb Sl
with Chilli and Choc

SERVES 4

4 lamb shanks
4 fresh red chillies, as hot or mild as you like
4 large garlic cloves (unpeeled)
8 shallots, peeled
1 medium aubergine, halved
1 tbsp oil
2 tbsp chopped marjoram or oregano
½ tsp ground cumin

½ tsp ground cinnamon
½ tsp coarsely ground black pepper
4 tbsp red wine vinegar
300ml red wine
300ml lamb or light chicken stock
2 tbsp redcurrant jelly
50g dark chocolate
½ tsp salt, or to taste

Trim the lamb shanks if necessary. Preheat the grill (or the oven to 220°C/Gas 7). Toss the chillies, garlic cloves, shallots and aubergine in the oil in the grill pan or a small roasting pan. Grill (or roast in the top of the oven) until charred and soft, removing each item once it is ready. Set the shallots aside for later.

Split the chillies, discard the seeds and stalks, then put them into a blender with the garlic and aubergine pulp. Add the marjoram, cumin, cinnamon and pepper. Blend to a paste, then spread all over the lamb shanks as evenly as possible. Put the shanks into a deep-sided roasting pan, into which they fit fairly snugly in one layer. Cover and leave to marinate in the fridge overnight.

The following day, preheat the oven to 150°C/Gas 2. Put the wine vinegar, wine, stock and redcurrant jelly in a pan, bring to the boil and let bubble until reduced by about one third. Uncover the lamb shanks, then pour the reduced liquor into the roasting pan. Tuck the shallots in too. Cover with a lid or foil, and slow-roast for 4–5 hours. The meat must be meltingly tender and falling off the bone.

Put the lamb shanks and the now-collapsed shallots into a serving dish. Skim off any fat from the juices in the pan. If the remaining sauce is still a bit thin, boil to reduce down, stirring as you do so, until it is rich and thick. Stir in the chocolate and add salt to taste. Pour the sauce over the meat and serve.

This is a rich Mexican dish with European influences, which I serve with quinoa, couscous, mash or rice. It is essentially a winter dish, but a salsa of chopped mango, red onion and lots of fresh coriander on the side turns it into one that works in summer too. You can go easier on the chilli if you like. It's a dish that can be reheated successfully, and freezes well. You'll need to marinate the meat overnight.

Charles Campion's
Rich Venison Stew

SERVES 8

2kg lean casserole venison
500ml bottle strong bitter beer
2 celery sticks, finely chopped
4 onions, finely chopped
4–6 tbsp good olive oil
2 tbsp red wine vinegar

250ml well-reduced, homemade
  stock
75g dark chocolate (minimum
  70% cocoa solids), grated
salt and black pepper

Cut the venison into chunks. For the marinade, combine the beer, celery, one of the onions, a splash of olive oil and the wine vinegar in a large bowl. Add the venison and toss to coat, then cover with cling film and leave to marinate in the fridge for 24 hours.

To cook the stew the next day, preheat the oven to 180°C/Gas 4. Heat the rest of the oil in a frying pan, add the remaining onions and fry until softened. Transfer to a large casserole dish, using a slotted spoon.

Pick the meat out of the marinade and seal, a few pieces at a time, in the oil remaining in the pan, then add to the casserole. Strain the marinade through a fine sieve and pour into the casserole. Finally pour in the stock. Cover and cook in the oven for 1½–2 hours or until the meat is tender.

Take out the casserole and turn the oven off. Drain the liquor through a sieve into a saucepan, retaining the meat in the casserole dish. Cover the casserole and place in the oven to keep warm.

Boil the liquor rapidly until reduced to the desired consistency – I think it should coat the back of a spoon. Then stir in the chocolate to 'polish' the sauce. Now, and only now, should you season the sauce with salt and pepper. When it is to your liking, pour the sauce back over the venison. Serve immediately, with steamed cabbage or green beans and creamy mash.

To enjoy venison at its best, use a good marinade and cook the meat in a casserole with a rich sauce. This overcomes the tendency for this lean meat to be tough and dry. Good bitter chocolate is the key to success here. You would find it hard to identify in the finished dish, but it gives you a dark, glossy sauce that is robust enough to hold its own with the richness of the meat.

chocolate tasting

Teatime

One of the last sanctuaries of gentler times, there's nothing that refreshes the spirits quite like teatime. So whether you're enjoying the spontaneous visit of a friend or staging something a little more ambitious, these recipes will make sure your guests are suitably occupied while you pour the Darjeeling. Using your best porcelain of course.

Alex Barker's
Florentines

MAKES 10–18

50g butter, plus extra to grease
75g caster sugar
2 tbsp double cream
110g slivered almonds

2 tbsp plain flour
2 tbsp chopped candied peel
2 tbsp chopped glacé cherries
110g dark or white chocolate

Preheat the oven to 180°C/Gas 4. Grease one or two baking sheets. Melt the butter and sugar together in a heavy-based pan over a low heat until the sugar has dissolved, then add the cream. Stir well and let the mixture boil for a minute. Take off the heat and add the almonds, flour, candied peel and glacé cherries, mixing thoroughly.

Drop small spoonfuls of the mixture, well apart, onto greased baking sheets. Bake for about 10 minutes until golden brown. Leave on the baking sheets for a few minutes, then transfer to a wire rack and leave until cold. Meanwhile melt the chocolate (see page 13) and let cool slightly.

Spread one side of the biscuits with the melted chocolate and mark patterns with a fork. Leave until set. Store in an airtight tin for up to 3 or 4 days.

Scrumptious Italian
chocolate-coated candied fruit and almond biscuits that are easy to make – but be warned, they are likely to disappear fast! Make them bite size or bigger, as you like. Coat with dark or white chocolate, or half with each as I have here.

Diana Henry's
Chocolate Ginger Tiffin

MAKES ABOUT 8

225g ginger biscuits
125g butter
2 tbsp golden syrup
1½ tbsp cocoa powder
50g sultanas or raisins

75g blanched almonds or
   hazelnuts, toasted and
   broken into pieces
200g dark chocolate, in pieces

Crush the ginger biscuits in a food processor, using the pulse button, or by putting them in a plastic bag and bashing them with a rolling pin. You want to end up with a mixture that is a blend of completely crushed biscuits and small chunks.

Melt the butter and golden syrup together in a heavy-based pan over a low heat. Add the cocoa powder, dried fruit and nuts, and stir until everything comes together. Press the mixture into a baking tin, about 16cm square, and let it cool, then refrigerate until set.

For the topping, melt the chocolate (see page 13), then pour over the tiffin and spread evenly. Leave to set. Once it is firm, cut the tiffin into squares or bars.

A superior chocolate
biscuit cake, which is a doddle to make. Serve it at teatime, or with little cups of strong espresso as a mid-morning snack, or as an alternative to a pudding.

Kate Whiteman's
Chocolate Shortbread

MAKES ABOUT 36

250g plain flour
25g cocoa powder
250g unsalted butter, at room
   temperature
95g icing sugar, sifted

1 large egg white
110g dark, bitter chocolate
   (70% cocoa solids), melted
   (see page 13), optional

Sift the flour and cocoa powder together. Beat the butter in a bowl, using a hand-held electric mixer until pale and fluffy. Add the icing sugar and egg white, and beat for a minute until well combined. Add the flour and cocoa mixture and mix on a low speed until just incorporated. Cover and chill until the dough is firm.

Divide the dough in half. Place each portion on a sheet of cling film or baking parchment and roll it into a cylinder, about 4cm in diameter. Wrap tightly and refrigerate until firm.

Preheat the oven to 180°C/Gas 4. Line two baking sheets with baking parchment. Cut the dough into 1cm slices and place on the baking sheets, spacing them well apart. Bake for 15–18 minutes until firm, then cool on a wire rack.

Serve the shortbreads either as they are, or dip one half of each in melted chocolate and leave to set on a sheet of baking parchment.

Crumbly shortbreads
which are perfect to nibble with a cup of coffee, tea or hot chocolate. Serve plain or dipped in dark chocolate, as you like.

These cookies keep well in an airtight container for up to 4 days and they make great lunchbox treats. Other nuts, such as walnuts or pecans, can be used instead of macadamias.

Fudgy-wudgy Cookies
Australian Women's Weekly

MAKES 24

125g butter, in pieces
1 tsp vanilla extract
250g brown sugar
1 egg
150g plain flour
35g self-raising flour
1 tsp bicarbonate of soda

35g cocoa powder
85g raisins
100g macadamia nuts, toasted
  and coarsely chopped
95g dark chocolate buttons or
  chocolate chips
100g dark chocolate, chopped

Preheat the oven to 180°C/Gas 4. Line three baking trays with baking parchment.

Beat the butter, vanilla extract, sugar and egg together, using an electric mixer (or hand-held electric beater) until smooth.

Sift the flours, bicarbonate of soda and cocoa powder together and stir into the mixture. Finally mix in the raisins, chopped nuts and all of the chocolate.

Drop rounded tablespoons of the mixture onto the prepared baking trays, spacing them about 4cm apart. Press each round lightly with the back of a fork to flatten it slightly. Bake in the oven for about 10 minutes.

Leave the cookies on the baking trays for 5 minutes to firm up, then transfer to a wire rack to cool.

Annie Bell's
Truffle Cupcakes

MAKES ABOUT 14

25g cocoa powder
100ml boiling water
50g unsalted butter, in pieces
100g golden caster sugar
1 medium egg
85g plain flour
½ tsp bicarbonate of soda
¼ tsp baking powder

ICING:
100g dark chocolate (about
  75% cocoa solids), in pieces
100ml double cream

TO FINISH:
dark (or milk) chocolate
  shavings (see page 15)

Heat the oven to 190°C/Gas 5. Place 14 paper cases in two fairy cake trays. Put the cocoa powder into a small bowl, pour on the boiling water and whisk until smooth, then leave to cool.

Cream the butter and sugar together in a food processor until pale. Beat in the egg, then sift in the dry ingredients and fold in. Finally incorporate the blended cocoa.

Half-fill the paper cake cases with the mixture and bake in the oven for about 17 minutes or until the cakes are risen and springy to the touch. Leave in the tins for a few minutes, then transfer to a wire rack to cool.

For the icing, put the chocolate into a heatproof bowl. Bring the cream to the boil in a small pan and pour onto the chocolate. Leave for a few minutes, then stir to melt the chocolate. Leave for a few minutes longer, then stir again – you should have a thick glossy cream. (If the chocolate hasn't completely melted, set the bowl over a pan of simmering water and stir until smooth.)

Drop a teaspoonful of icing onto each cake and spread with a small palette knife. Scatter over some chocolate shavings and set aside for about 1 hour to set.

Deeply, darkly chocolatey – these cupcakes are a little bit more bitter than usual – with an icing that is pure chocolate truffle.

Little almond cakes dotted with dark chocolate that can be baked a day ahead.

Mini Choc Chip Friands
Australian Women's Weekly

MAKES 18

90g butter, melted, plus extra
   to grease
3 egg whites
60g ground almonds
120g icing sugar, sifted
35g plain flour, sifted
100g dark chocolate, finely
   chopped

TOPPING:
60ml double cream
100g dark chocolate, in pieces

Preheat the oven to 180°C/Gas 4. Lightly grease two 12-hole mini muffin tins.

Lightly whisk the egg whites in a bowl with a fork until combined. Add the butter, ground almonds, icing sugar and flour and stir with a wooden spoon until just combined. Finally stir in the chopped chocolate.

Spoon tablespoonfuls of the mixture into the muffin moulds and bake in the oven for about 15 minutes or until lightly browned and cooked through. Turn out onto wire racks to cool.

For the topping, put the cream and chocolate in a heatproof bowl over a pan of simmering water until the chocolate has just melted, stirring until smooth. Take off the heat and leave to cool until thickened. Spoon the creamy chocolate on top of the friands and leave to set before serving.

Mary Gwynn's

Choc-nut Brownies

with grilled strawberries

SERVES 8

100g butter, diced, plus extra
  to grease
50g dark chocolate, in pieces
2 eggs
few drops of vanilla extract
50g self-raising flour
½ tsp baking powder
pinch of salt
175g granulated sugar
100g unsalted cashew nuts or
  macademia nuts
50g white chocolate, cut into
small chunks

GRILLED STRAWBERRIES:
450g strawberries, hulled
15g butter
1 tbsp clear honey

Soft, gooey, nutty brownies served with honey-glazed strawberries… what could be more tempting?

Preheat the oven to 180°C/Gas 4. Butter and line an 18 x 28cm baking tin (one that's not too shallow) with baking parchment. Melt the butter and chocolate in a heatproof bowl set over a pan of gently simmering water. Stir until melted, take off the heat and let cool slightly.

Beat the eggs with the vanilla extract. Sift the flour, baking powder and salt together onto the eggs, add the sugar and beat well. Lightly mix in the cashew nuts and white chocolate, then fold into the melted chocolate mixture.

Spoon the mixture into the prepared tin and spread level. Bake in the oven for 25–30 minutes until the mixture is just firm to the touch and a skewer inserted in the middle emerges with a little of the still-sticky mixture and a few crumbs clinging to it. Leave in the tin for 5 minutes, then remove and cut into 8 squares. Cool on a wire rack.

For the strawberries, preheat the grill. Thread the berries onto short wooden skewers. Melt the butter with the honey over a low heat and brush over the strawberries. Grill, turning occasionally, until browned. Serve with the brownies.

Galton Blackiston's
Financiers
with chocolate orange centres

MAKES 24

FINANCIERS:
150g unsalted butter, plus extra
    to grease
25g plain flour, plus extra to dust
110g ground almonds
60g caster sugar
3 egg whites
25ml golden syrup

CHOCOLATE ORANGE FILLING:
40g milk chocolate, in pieces
25g dark chocolate, in pieces
65ml double cream
25ml golden syrup
1 tbsp Cointreau or other
    orange liqueur
10g unsalted butter

Preheat the oven to 190°C/Gas 5. Lightly butter and flour two 12-hole mini muffin trays.

Now make the chocolate and orange filling. Put the milk and dark chocolates into a bowl. Bring the cream and golden syrup to the boil in a saucepan, then pour onto the chocolate, stirring constantly until it has melted. Add the liqueur and butter, and stir vigorously until really smooth. Set aside to cool.

To make the financiers, combine the flour, ground almonds and sugar in a bowl. Add the egg whites and golden syrup, and mix thoroughly. Leave to rest while you prepare the butter.

Melt the butter in a saucepan, then cook over a moderate heat until it is a light nut-brown colour. Immediately take off the heat and set aside to cool. When it is cold, stir the brown butter into the rested cake mixture.

Spoon the mixture into the prepared mini muffin tins and bake on the top shelf of the oven for 10–12 minutes, or until risen and golden. Set aside to cool slightly, for a few minutes.

Put the chocolate orange filling into a piping bag fitted with a fine plain nozzle and, while the financiers are still warm, pipe a little into the centre of each one through the top. Serve immediately.

Elegant little cakes to serve for afternoon tea, or as petits fours. You can make the filling ahead for convenience, but bring back to room temperature before piping.

Joanna Farrow's
White Chocolate Scones
with strawberry and pink peppercorn butter

MAKES 10

225g self-raising flour
2 tsp baking powder
25g icing sugar
40g unsalted butter, diced
150g white chocolate, finely
  chopped
125ml milk, plus extra to glaze

STRAWBERRY BUTTER:

200g small, firm strawberries
125g unsalted butter, softened
3 tbsp icing sugar
2 tsp crushed pink peppercorns

Preheat the oven to 220°C/Gas 7. Grease a large baking sheet.

First make the strawberry butter. Thinly slice the strawberries and pat dry between several sheets of kitchen paper. Whisk the butter with the icing sugar and peppercorns until pale and creamy. Gently stir in the strawberries and turn into a small dish. Cover and chill.

To make the scones, whiz the flour, baking powder and icing sugar in a food processor with the butter until the mixture resembles fine breadcrumbs. Add the chocolate and milk and mix to a soft dough.

On a floured surface, gently roll out the dough to a 2cm thickness. Cut out rounds, using a 5–6cm cutter and place on the baking sheet. Brush the tops with milk to glaze and bake in the oven for 10–12 minutes until risen and golden. Transfer to a wire rack. Serve warm or cold, with the strawberry butter.

Dress up simple scones with lavish amounts of chopped white chocolate and serve freshly baked – with a generous topping of creamy strawberry butter spiked with crushed pink peppercorns.

Sarah Jane Evans'
Midnight Meringues

MAKES ABOUT 30

2 egg whites
120g caster sugar
1 tsp vanilla extract
120g pecans or walnuts, coarsely chopped

150g dark chocolate (60–70% cocoa solids), roughly chopped
whipped cream or chocolate ganache (see page 15), to serve (optional)

Preheat the oven to 180°C/Gas 4. Line two baking sheets with non-stick baking parchment.

Whisk the egg whites in a clean, dry bowl until they hold stiff peaks. Gradually whisk in the sugar, a spoonful at a time, to make a firm, glossy meringue. Using a metal spoon, fold in the vanilla extract, nuts and chocolate.

Place heaped teaspoonfuls of the meringue on the prepared baking sheets. Put them into the oven and immediately turn it off. Do not open the door, but leave the meringues inside overnight to dry.

The following morning, peel them carefully away from the sheets and store in an airtight container until required.

Serve plain, or sandwiched together in pairs with whipped cream or chocolate ganache.

Delightfully crunchy
small meringues, which conveniently dry out slowly in the oven overnight – hence their name. They are perfect for afternoon tea or late party food. Choose a really good chocolate that's not too dark – you want an element of creaminess.

Anne Willan's
Chocolate Tartlets
with candied orange

MAKES 8

PASTRY:

175g plain flour, plus extra
   to dust

½ tsp salt

100g caster sugar

3 medium egg yolks

1 tsp vanilla extract

100g butter, in pieces, slightly
   softened

FILLING:

4 oranges

150g sugar

250g dark chocolate (about 60%
   cocoa solids), chopped

125ml double cream

90g butter

2 tbsp Grand Marnier

To make the pastry, sift the flour into a mound on the work surface and make a well in the centre. Put the salt, sugar, egg yolks, vanilla extract and butter into the well and work these ingredients together with the fingertips of one hand until thoroughly mixed and the sugar is partially dissolved. Gradually draw in the flour until the dough comes together, then knead lightly until smooth. Shape into a ball, wrap in cling film and chill until firm, at least 30 minutes.

Meanwhile, prepare the filling. Pare the zest from the oranges with a swivel peeler and cut into fine julienne strips, using a large knife. Put the orange zest strips in a pan of cold water, bring to the boil and simmer for 5 minutes, then drain.

Squeeze the juice from the oranges and pour into a saucepan. Add the sugar and heat gently until dissolved, then bring to the boil and simmer for 2 minutes. Add the julienne zest and lower the heat. Simmer very gently, without stirring, until the zests are translucent and very tender, and almost all the liquid has evaporated; this will take 30–40 minutes. If the pan appears to be becoming dry before they are done, add a little water. Lift out the julienne with a slotted spoon, spread them on a sheet of baking parchment and leave to cool and dry. Strain the syrup and set 2 tbsp aside in a small pan.

Heat the oven to 190°C/Gas 5 and butter eight 8cm tartlet tins. Divide the dough into 8 pieces. Shape each one into a ball, roll out to a 10cm round and trim the edges with a 10cm pastry cutter. Line the tartlet tins with the pastry rounds, pressing well into the base. Prick the bases with a fork and chill until firm, about 15 minutes.

If you have more tartlet tins, place a second one in each pastry case, so it keeps its shape during baking. Otherwise, line the cases with greaseproof paper and dried beans or rice to weight down. Set the tins on a baking sheet and bake for 6–8 minutes until the pastry is set and the rims start to colour. Remove the lining tins or paper and beans and bake for a further 5–7 minutes until the cases are golden brown and cooked. Leave to cool in the tins, then carefully remove.

To assemble, reserve about 2 tbsp of the orange zest julienne for decoration. Chop the rest, and spread evenly in the tartlet cases.

For the ganache filling, tip the chocolate into a small bowl. Put the cream, butter and reserved 2 tbsp orange syrup into a pan and heat gently until the butter is melted. Bring just to the boil, then pour onto the chocolate and let stand for 1 minute until melted. Stir the mixture until smooth, then stir in the Grand Marnier.

Pour this ganache into the tartlet cases, covering the orange zest completely and filling the cases almost to the rim. Tap gently on the work surface to level the ganache. Leave the tartlets at room temperature until set, about 30 minutes, but don't refrigerate. Just before serving, top with the reserved candied orange zest.

Candied orange zest

and a luscious dark chocolate ganache form the filling for these stunning tartlets. Serve them within a few hours of making – for afternoon tea or as an indulgent dessert.

Michael Smith's
Chocolate Pye

To make the pastry, sift the flour and salt into a bowl, add the butter and toss to coat in the flour. Lightly rub the flour and butter together, using your fingertips until you have a moist sand-like texture. Stir in the sugar. Make a well, using a large fork. Beat the egg yolk and water together and pour into the well. Work the ingredients together with your fingers, then gather the dough into a loose ball.

Knead the pastry lightly and quickly (just two or three quick kneads are enough) to incorporate everything into a soft pad. Wrap in a cloth or greaseproof paper and leave the pastry to relax in the fridge or cool larder for 30 minutes.

Butter a deep 22.5cm flan tin or ring placed on a baking sheet. Lightly flour a marble slab, board or work surface. Form the pastry into a round of even thickness, then lightly flour the rolling pin and roll out the pastry to a circle large enough to line the flan tin. Using the rolling pin, lift the pastry into the tin and gently press into the edges. Trim off the excess pastry overhanging the rim. Cover with greaseproof paper and rest in the fridge for 20 minutes. Meanwhile, preheat the oven to 220°C/Gas 7.

Line the pastry case with greaseproof paper and baking beans and bake blind for 10 minutes. Lower the oven setting to 190°C/Gas 5 and bake for a further 8 minutes. Remove the beans and paper and return to the oven for a further 8 minutes until the pastry is cooked and golden. Allow to cool.

To make the filling, put the chocolate, sherry or rum and 6 tbsp water in a heatproof bowl and set over a pan of simmering water. (If you are using sherry, add the vanilla extract.) Leave until the chocolate has melted and the mixture is quite hot. Meanwhile, soften the gelatine in 2 tbsp cold water.

Add the gelatine to the hot chocolate mixture and stir well, making sure it is totally dissolved. Remove the bowl from the heat and beat in the egg yolks, one by one. Leave until cool but not set.

Whisk the egg whites in a clean bowl until they form firm peaks, then cut and fold these through the chocolate mixture until evenly incorporated. Tip the filling into the pastry case and gently smooth the surface. Allow to set in a cool place, but do not refrigerate (or the pastry will go soggy).

To serve, decorate with piped swirls of whipped cream and crystallised rose petals or violets.

SERVES 8–10

PASTRY:
225g plain flour, plus extra
　to dust
½ tsp salt
140g butter, diced
55g caster sugar
1 egg yolk
2 tbsp water

FILLING:
280g dark chocolate, in pieces
4 tbsp sherry or rum
8 tbsp cold water
1 tsp vanilla extract (optional)
1 tsp powdered gelatine
5 eggs, separated

TO DECORATE:
whipped cream
crystallised rose petals or violets

This chocolate tart has appeared in various guises, many times from my pen and kitchen. This particular version is relatively easy to make. It's very rich, however, so you should serve only a small slice.

Alex Mackay's
Chocolate, Orange and Pine Nut Tart

SERVES 6

CHOCOLATE SHORTBREAD PASTRY:
80g unsalted butter
50g icing sugar, plus extra to dust
1 egg yolk
80g plain flour, plus extra to dust
40g cocoa powder
2 tbsp cold water

ORANGE ZEST AND SYRUP:
4 oranges
salt
200g caster sugar

FILLING:
75g dark chocolate (72% cocoa solids), chopped
50g unsalted butter, diced
4 eggs, separated
50g caster sugar
40g cocoa powder, sifted
50g pine nuts

Pine nuts and tangy oranges balance the richness of this irresistible sticky chocolate mousse tart.

For the chocolate shortbread pastry, mix all the ingredients together until smooth, either by hand or in the food processor (the dough will seem very wet). Flour your hands well and shape the mixture into a flat circle. Wrap it in cling film and chill for at least 30 minutes to firm up before rolling.

Pare the zest from the oranges in long, fine wide strips, using a swivel peeler and set aside. Next, peel away all the white pith. Segment the oranges over a bowl to catch the juice and squeeze the juice from the membranes, too. Put the segments to one side.

Blanch the orange zests in a pan of salted water for 1 minute, then refresh under cold running water. Repeat this process, then put the zests into a small pan with the reserved juice and the sugar (but not the segments). Simmer over a low heat for about 10 minutes until the zests are translucent. Remove with a slotted spoon and lay half of them on a piece of greaseproof paper. Chop the other half as finely as possible and put into a small bowl. Add the orange segments to the remaining syrup and reserve for serving.

Preheat the oven to 190°C/Gas 5. Set a 20cm flan ring on a baking sheet. To roll out the pastry, place it on a large sheet of floured cling film on your work surface. Dust the pastry with flour and top with another sheet of cling film. Roll out to a round slightly larger than your flan ring, giving the pastry a quarter-turn between rollings to ensure an even thickness. Chill for about 15 minutes.

Remove the top layer of cling film and drape the pastry over your rolling pin. Lift it over the top of the flan ring, with the other layer of cling film uppermost. Ease the pastry into the sides of the tin before pressing down the edges. Remove the cling film.

For the filling, melt the chocolate in a heatproof bowl over a pan of barely simmering water. Stir in the butter and reserved chopped orange zest, then remove from the heat.

Whisk the egg whites in a clean bowl until firm, then gradually whisk in the sugar a tablespoonful at a time, and continue whisking until stiff. Fold in the lightly beaten egg yolks, then gently fold in the cocoa powder with a spatula. Take a third of this mixture and stir it vigorously into the still-warm chocolate. Carefully fold this into the remaining whisked egg white, then turn the mixture into the lined flan ring.

Sprinkle the pine nuts over the filling and bake in the oven for 20–25 minutes until firm around the outside, but still slightly runny in the centre. Transfer the tart to a wire rack and allow to cool for 10 minutes before removing the ring. Let cool to room temperature, but don't refrigerate.

When ready to serve, dust generously with icing sugar and top with the reserved candied orange zests. Serve accompanied by the orange segments in syrup.

Linda Sue's
Chocolate Cheesecake

SERVES 10–12

CRUST:
335g digestive biscuits
175g butter
2 tbsp ground almonds
225g vanilla caster sugar (see
    page 15), or 225g sugar and
    ½ tsp vanilla extract

FILLING:
450g full-fat soft cream cheese
    (e.g. Philadelphia)
60g caster sugar
3 eggs, well beaten
150ml double cream
150g dark chocolate

TOPPING:
330ml soured cream
2 tbsp caster sugar

Preheat the oven to 220°C/Gas 7. Have ready a 33cm x 23cm roasting tin or shallow baking tin with similar dimensions.

For the crust, crush the biscuits with a rolling pin. Melt the butter, then mix together with the crushed biscuits, ground almonds and vanilla sugar. Tip into the roasting tin, spread evenly and pack very firmly with a fork to line the bottom and part way up the sides to form a crust. Chill.

For the filling, cream the soft cheese and sugar together in a bowl until smooth. Gradually mix in the eggs, blending thoroughly, then stir in the cream. Pour half of this mixture into the chilled crust.

Melt the chocolate and stir into the remaining filling. Dollop into the crust, marbling the chocolate and vanilla mixtures together with a knife. Bake in the oven for 30 minutes until the filling is set. Allow to cool. Increase the oven setting to 220°C/Gas 7.

For the topping, mix the soured cream and sugar together, then spread evenly over the cheesecake. Bake for 5–8 minutes to form a glaze. Chill for several hours. Remove from the fridge an hour or two before serving.

Rich and gorgeous, the recipe for this compact, marbled chocolate cheesecake was sent to Jeremy Round at the Independent by Linda Sue Park, the first winner of the newspaper's cookery competition. Try it!

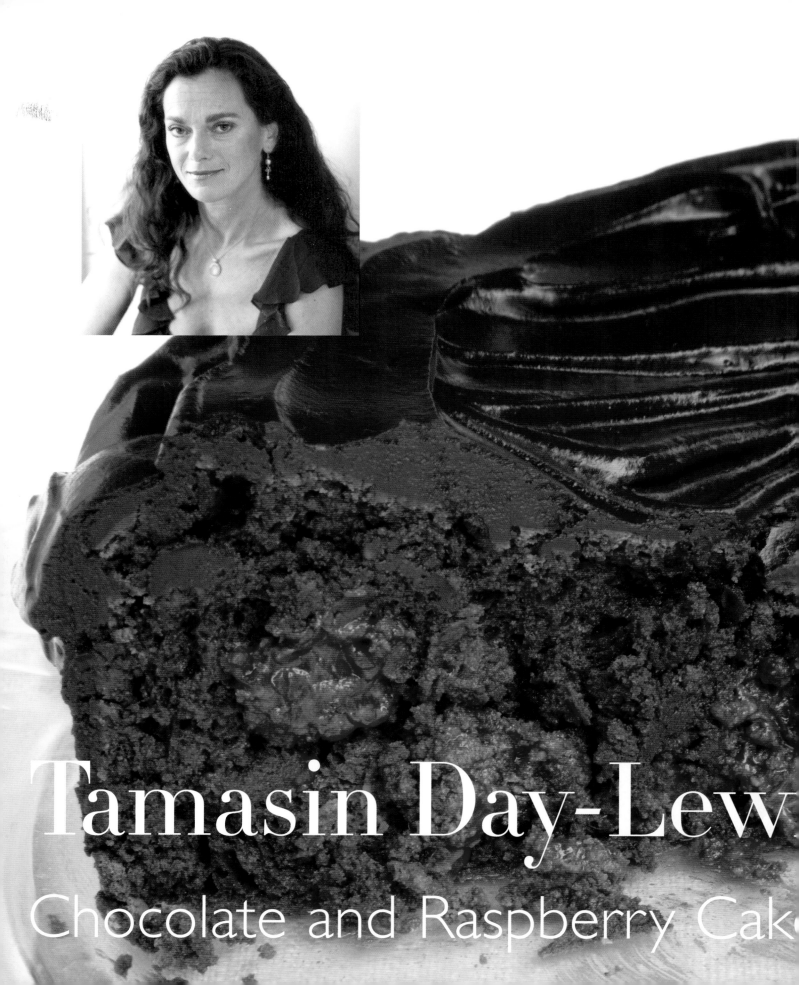

Tamasin Day-Lew

Chocolate and Raspberry Cak

This is a magical cake, which you can make without the raspberries if you are of a purist chocoholic bent, or simply don't agree with chocolate and fruit, which some don't. The cake is flourless, but moist with freshly ground almonds. Make it a day or two in advance if you like and store in a tin, applying the ganache before serving.

SERVES 8–10

butter, to grease
flour, to dust
4 eggs, separated, plus 1 whole
   egg
170g vanilla caster sugar (see
   page 15)
225g dark, bitter chocolate
   (minimum 70% cocoa solids)

140g blanched almonds, freshly
   ground
1 heaped tsp ground coffee
200g raspberries

Ganache:
120ml double cream
225g dark chocolate

Preheat the oven to 170°C/Gas 3. Grease and flour a 20cm spring-form cake tin and line the base with buttered greaseproof paper.

Whisk the egg yolks and whole egg together with half the sugar using an electric mixer (or a hand-held electric beater), until pale and doubled in volume. Melt the chocolate (see page 13) and let cool slightly.

Whisk the egg whites in a clean bowl until they form peaks, then whisk in the remaining sugar a spoonful at a time, until it is all incorporated and the mixture forms soft peaks.

Add half of the egg whites to the whisked egg and sugar mixture and fold in gently. Add the melted chocolate and the rest of the whites, folding as you go. Then do the same with the ground almonds and coffee. Last of all, add the raspberries and fold in with extreme gentleness to avoid breaking them up.

Spoon the mixture into the prepared tin and bake in the oven for 30 minutes. Turn the oven off and leave the cake inside to cook in the residual heat for another 15 minutes, or until a skewer inserted into the centre comes out clean. Remove from the oven and leave to cool in the tin, then place on a wire rack over a tray.

To make the ganache slowly heat the cream until it is about to come to the boil, then take off the heat. Add the chocolate and stir until melted and smooth. Spread the ganache all over the cake and leave to cool and set before serving.

Jane Suthering's
Chocolate marble cake

ABOUT 12 SLICES

melted butter, to grease tin
250g golden caster sugar, plus
    extra to sprinkle
250g butter, softened
4 large eggs, beaten
250g self-raising flour, sifted
finely grated zest of 1 orange
55g chopped mixed peel

2 tbsp orange juice, or 1 tbsp
    orange liqueur plus 1 tbsp
    dark rum
2 tbsp cocoa powder, sifted
85g dark chocolate, coarsely
    chopped
icing sugar, to dust

Preheat the oven to 180°C/Gas 4. Thoroughly brush the inside of a 23cm diameter (1.75 litre capacity) kugelhopf tin with melted butter, then sprinkle with caster sugar until evenly coated. Shake out any excess.

In a large bowl, cream the butter and sugar together until the mixture is a soft dropping consistency, then beat in the eggs, a little at a time, until thoroughly incorporated. Fold in the sifted flour and divide the mixture into two equal portions.

Add the orange zest, mixed peel and half the orange juice (or the liqueur) to one half. Mix the remaining orange juice (or the rum) with the cocoa until smooth, then stir this into the other half, together with the chopped chocolate.

Drop alternate spoonfuls of the mixtures into the prepared tin until all the mixture is used. Tap the tin sharply on the worktop to level the surface. Bake in the oven for about 1 hour, until well risen and firm to the touch.

Leave the cake to cool until the tin can be handled comfortably, then shake it to loosen the cake. Unmould and place the cake upright on a wire rack, then replace the tin on top and leave until completely cold. Store in an airtight container or wrap in foil to prevent it from drying out.

Dust the cake with icing sugar before serving, cut into slices.

A lovely moist cake that keeps beautifully in an airtight container, ready to 'cut and come again'.

Marie-Pierre Moine's
Chocolate Cake Maison

8–10 SLICES
200g dark chocolate, in pieces
2 tbsp water
140g caster sugar
150g unsalted butter, softened,
    plus extra to grease
2 tbsp self-raising flour
1 tbsp ground almonds
5 medium eggs, separated
small pinch of salt
dash of Cointreau (optional)

COATING:
150g dark, bitter chocolate, in
    pieces
100ml single cream

Melt the chocolate with the water in a large heavy-based saucepan over a very low heat, stirring frequently with a wooden spoon. Stir in the sugar and take the pan off the heat while you cut the butter into small pieces. Return to a very low heat and stir in the butter, a little at a time. Now sift in the flour, add the ground almonds and stir lightly to combine. Cook, stirring gently, for a minute, still over a low heat, then take off the hob and let the mixture cool a little.

Meanwhile, heat the oven to 170°C/Gas 3. Generously butter a 900g loaf tin or 20cm round cake tin.

Beat the egg yolks into the mixture one at a time. In a clean bowl, whisk the egg whites with the salt until very firm. Using a large metal spoon, carefully fold them into the chocolate mixture until evenly incorporated, working lightly, with upward movements. Fold in the liqueur if using.

Tip the mixture into the greased tin and tap it gently on the work surface a couple of times to level the mixture. Bake in the oven for about 45 minutes. Resist opening the oven door to check on the cake for the first 25 minutes. The cake is ready when it is firm, but still a little soft in the centre.

Leave to cool in the tin for 15 minutes or so, then carefully remove and place on a wire rack. Leave to cool completely before coating.

For the coating, melt the chocolate with the cream in a saucepan over a very low heat, stirring frequently with a wooden spoon. Remove from the heat and leave to cool. Set the cooling rack over a platter (to catch the drips), then pour the coating on top of the cake. Use a small palette knife to smooth it evenly over the top and sides. Leave to set for 1 hour before serving.

Dark, rich ... just as a home-made chocolate cake should be. It keeps well for several days in the fridge wrapped loosely in foil.

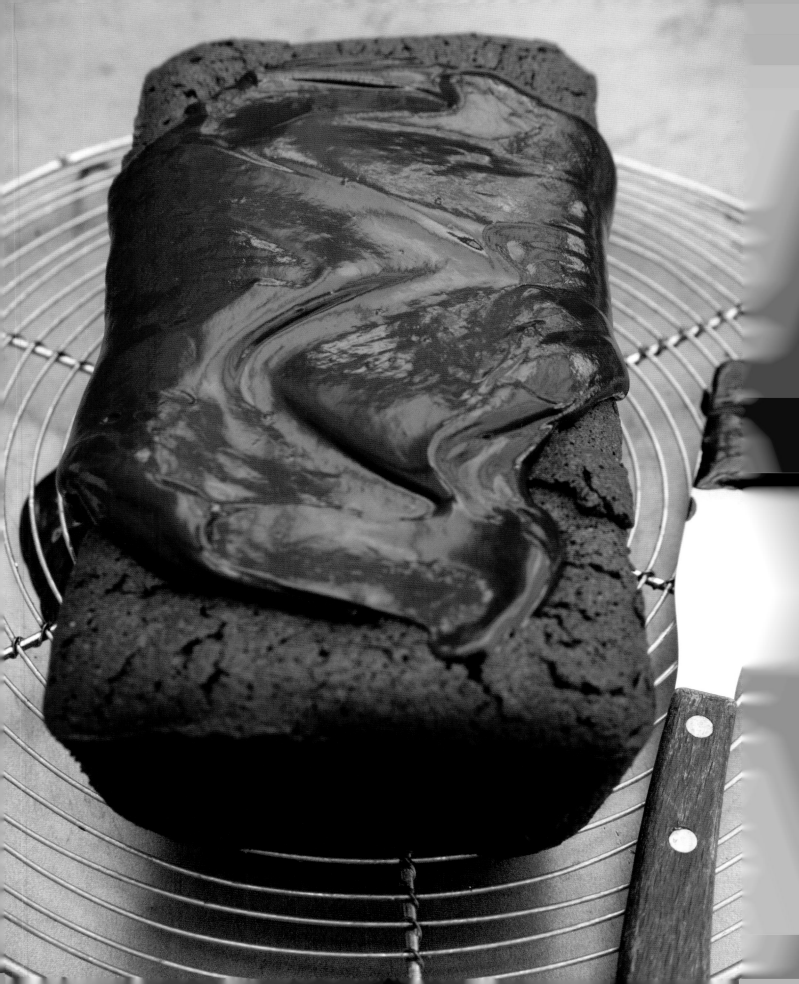

Patrick Anthony's
Favourite Chocolate Cake

ABOUT 12 SLICES

a little oil, to grease tin
225g dark chocolate (ideally 70% cocoa solids), in pieces
110g butter
225g caster sugar
4 large eggs
3 tbsp whisky, rum or orange liqueur
2 heaped tbsp plain flour

50g walnuts or pecans, chopped (optional)
cocoa powder and/or icing sugar, to dust

RASPBERRY ICE CREAM (OPTIONAL):
125g frozen raspberries
300ml double cream
80g icing sugar

Preheat the oven to 190°C/Gas 5. Lightly oil a 23cm springform cake tin, at least 8cm deep.

Melt the chocolate and butter together in a heavy-based saucepan over a very gentle heat, giving an occasional stir. Remove the pan from the heat and stir in the sugar. Next, add the eggs and beat into the mixture. Add your choice of booze, plus the flour and stir until well blended. Add the nuts if using and stir to distribute.

Pour the mixture into the prepared tin and bake in the centre of the oven for 30 minutes. (The cake will rise and sink back down and it might crack, but don't worry – this is normal.) Run a knife around the edge of the cake and leave in the tin for 10 minutes, then release the tin and place the cake on a wire rack to cool.

To make the raspberry ice cream if required, simply whiz the raspberries, cream and icing sugar together in a blender on full speed for about 10 seconds. It's ready to eat straight away, or you can freeze it – remembering to take it out about 20 minutes before serving to soften slightly.

To serve, dust the cake with sifted cocoa powder and/or icing sugar. Cut into thin slices and accompany with raspberry ice cream or double cream if you like. Leftovers, if any, will keep for a few days well wrapped in foil in an airtight container.

A dense, rich cake that is virtually foolproof. The only equipment needed to make it is a saucepan, a spoon and a 23cm cake tin. It also makes a great pudding – served with a dollop of my 'instant' raspberry ice cream or chilled double cream.

Henrietta Green's
Best-ever Chocolate Cake

8–10 SLICES
225g unsalted butter, plus extra
    to grease
225g dark chocolate, broken into
    pieces
225g caster sugar
6 eggs
225g ground hazelnuts
115g fresh brown or white
    breadcrumbs
grated zest of 1 orange

FILLING:
2 tbsp marmalade

GLAZE:
115g dark chocolate, in pieces
2 tsp clear honey
55g unsalted butter, diced

TO DECORATE (OPTIONAL):
30g white chocolate

Preheat the oven to 190°C/Gas 5. Generously grease two 21cm sandwich cake tins with butter and line the bases with discs of buttered greaseproof paper. Melt the chocolate (see page 13) and leave to cool slightly.

In a large bowl, cream the butter until smooth. Then whisk in the sugar, a little at a time, until the mixture is light and fluffy. Beat in the eggs, one at a time, beating well after each addition. If the mixture looks a little curdled, do not worry. Whisk the melted chocolate into the mixture, then stir in the hazelnuts and breadcrumbs, and finally the orange zest.

Spoon the mixture into the prepared tins, smooth the tops and bake in the oven for 20–25 minutes, until the centre is just firm to a light touch. As these cakes are quite fragile, allow them to cool in their tins.

Run a knife around the edge of the cakes, then turn one of them out onto a serving plate and remove the greaseproof paper disc. Lightly spread with a layer of marmalade. Carefully turn the other cake out onto a board, remove the paper, then place the cake on top of the other one.

To make the glaze, melt the chocolate, honey and butter in a heatproof bowl set over a pan of hot water on a medium-low heat and stir until smooth. Remove from the heat and continue beating the glaze as it cools until it thickens.

Pour the glaze on top of the cake and spread evenly all over with a spatula. Leave to set. If you want to decorate the cake, before the glaze has set hard, shave the white chocolate over the cake, using a vegetable peeler, allowing the chocolate slivers to fall on to the cake.

This is not self-promotion, but a claim that I make on behalf of Josceline Dimbleby, whose recipe this is. Not only is this a cake you cannot refuse, it is also incredibly easy. The secret, according to Jossie, is to make it with really fresh breadcrumbs, from a white or brown loaf.

Indulge your friends and family with this moist and fudgy chocolate cake – ideal for birthdays and other celebrations.

Angela Nilsen's
Ultimate Chocolate Cake

12–14 SLICES
200g butter, in pieces, plus extra
to grease
200g dark chocolate (about 60%
cocoa solids), in pieces
1 tbsp instant coffee granules
125ml cold water
85g self-raising flour
85g plain flour
¼ tsp bicarbonate of soda
200g light muscovado sugar
200g golden caster sugar
25g cocoa powder
3 medium eggs
75ml buttermilk

GANACHE:
200g dark chocolate
(as above), in small pieces
284ml carton double cream
2 tbsp golden caster sugar

TO DECORATE:
chocolate shavings (see page 15)
or grated chocolate

Preheat the oven to 160°C/ Gas 3. Butter a 20cm round cake tin (7.5cm deep) and line the base with greaseproof paper.

Put the chocolate and butter into a medium heavy-based pan. Mix the coffee granules with the water and pour into the pan. Warm over a low heat just until everything is melted; don't overheat. (Or melt in the microwave on medium for about 5 minutes, stirring halfway through.)

Meanwhile, combine the flours, bicarbonate of soda, sugars and cocoa powder in a big bowl, mixing with your hands to get rid of any lumps. Beat the eggs in another bowl and stir in the buttermilk. Now pour the melted chocolate and egg mixtures into the flour mix, stirring just until everything is well blended and you have a smooth, fairly runny consistency.

Pour the mixture into the prepared tin and bake in the oven for 1 hour 25 minutes – 1 hour 30 minutes or until the top feel firms and a skewer inserted in the centre comes out clean (don't worry if it cracks a bit). Leave to cool in the tin for 10 minutes (it may dip slightly, which is fine), then turn out onto a wire rack to cool completely.

To make the ganache, put the chocolate into a bowl. Pour the cream into a pan, add the sugar and heat until it is about to boil. Take off the heat and pour it onto the chocolate, stirring constantly. Continue to stir until the chocolate has melted and the mixture is smooth.

Cut the cake horizontally into three and sandwich the layers together with a little of the ganache. Pour the rest over the cake, letting it fall down the sides and smoothing with a palette knife. Decorate with a pile of chocolate shavings or grated chocolate.

This cake will keep moist and gooey in an airtight container in a cool place for 3–4 days.

Ganache and Nut

ten's Gateâu

This is a favourite recipe that I have made from time to time when entertaining. Originally I made it with pistachios, which I recommend if you can find some really fresh ones. Otherwise pecan nuts are a better option.

ABOUT 12 SLICES

115g pecan nuts
175g unsalted butter
175g caster sugar
2 tsp finely grated orange zest
3 large eggs, beaten
115g self-raising flour
½ tsp baking powder
50g ground almonds
1 tbsp Curaçao, Grand Marnier
   or orange juice

GANACHE:
175g dark chocolate (about 70%
   cocoa solids), in pieces
2 tbsp Curaçao, Grand Marnier
   or orange juice
150ml double cream
25g icing sugar, sifted, or to taste

TOPPING:
40–50g pecan nuts

Preheat the oven to 160°C/Gas 3. Line a 20cm round cake tin with baking parchment. Chop the nuts by hand or in a food processor until quite fine.

Cream the butter, sugar and orange zest together in a bowl until soft and light. Gradually beat in the eggs. Sift the flour, baking powder and ground almonds together over the mixture and fold in gently, together with the chopped pecans, until evenly blended. Lastly add the liqueur or orange juice.

Spoon the mixture into the prepared cake tin and gently level the surface. Bake for about 1 hour until firm. Leave in the tin for 5 minutes, then turn out onto a wire rack to cool.

Meanwhile, prepare the ganache. Melt the chocolate (see page 13). Take off the heat and gradually stir in the liqueur or orange juice. Allow to cool. Whip the cream in another bowl until it forms soft peaks, then blend in the cooled chocolate and icing sugar to taste.

Cut the cake horizontally into three layers. Sandwich them together with some of the ganache, saving a generous amount for the topping. Swirl the ganache over the top of the cake and decorate with the pecans. Allow to stand for several hours until the ganache becomes firm before serving.

Hugo Arnold's
Chocolate Orange Cake

10–12 SLICES
175g dark chocolate (70% cocoa
    solids), in pieces
175g unsalted butter
225g caster sugar
6 eggs, separated
finely grated zest of 3 oranges
150g self-raising flour, sifted
pinch of salt

GANACHE:
250ml double cream
225g dark chocolate (55% cocoa
    solids)
1–2 tbsp Cointreau

TO FINISH:
orange slices

Preheat the oven to 170°C/Gas 3. Line a 23cm round cake tin with greaseproof paper. Melt the chocolate (see page 13), then remove from the heat and set aside.

Beat the butter and sugar together in a bowl until light and fluffy, then gradually beat in the egg yolks. Stir in the melted chocolate and the orange zest, then fold in the flour. In a clean bowl, whisk the egg whites with the salt until stiff, then carefully fold them into the mixture.

Spoon the mixture into the prepared cake tin and bake in the oven for 35–40 minutes, until a skewer inserted in the centre comes out clean. Turn out and leave to cool on a wire rack.

To make the ganache, put all the ingredients into a bowl set over a pan of simmering water and leave until the chocolate has melted. Stir until smooth, then remove from the heat and set aside for 10–20 minutes.

Pour the ganache onto the cake and smooth over the top and sides, using a palette knife. Decorate with orange slices to serve.

Richly flavoured with dark chocolate and tangy orange zest, this gorgeous cake is topped with a Cointreau-spiked ganache and fresh orange slices.

Desserts

Utterly irresistible, gorgeously gooey and wickedly tempting, there are very few in this world who can resist the seductive charms of a chocolate dessert. One stolen glance and we're lost, captivated and seduced. So whatever the time of day resistance is futile – give yourself over and enjoy these, our best-loved recipes.

The Pudding Club's
Steamed Chocolate Pudding
with fudge nut topping

SERVES 4–6

120g butter, plus extra to grease
120g soft brown sugar
2 eggs, beaten
90g self-raising flour
2 heaped tbsp cocoa powder

FUDGE NUT CHOCOLATE TOPPING:
180g dark chocolate, in pieces
1 tbsp caster sugar
5 tbsp single cream
60g mixed nuts, toasted

Butter a 1.7 litre pudding basin. To prepare the topping, melt the chocolate (see page 13), then remove from the heat and stir in the sugar, cream and nuts. Spoon the mixture into the bottom of the pudding basin.

For the sponge, beat the butter and brown sugar together in a bowl until light and fluffy. Gradually add the eggs, beating all the time. Sift the flour and cocoa powder together over the mixture and fold in carefully.

Turn the sponge mixture into the basin. Cover the top of the basin with a double thickness of greaseproof paper, making a pleat in the middle to allow for expansion. Secure under the rim with string.

Place the pudding basin in a steamer or stand on a trivet in a saucepan containing enough boiling water to come about halfway up the side. Cover tightly and steam for 1½ hours, topping up with more boiling water as necessary.

Turn the pudding out onto a warmed plate and serve with chocolate sauce (see page 15) or pouring cream.

Sheer indulgence for chocolate lovers – a moist dark chocolate sponge topped with its own delicious nutty fudge sauce.

Michel Roux's
Marbled Peppermint and
Chocolate Soufflés

These refreshing soufflés are really special. The flavour of peppermint with pockets of melted chocolate is surprising and irresistible.

SERVES 4

30g softened butter
150g caster sugar, plus an extra 30g to dust the dishes
50ml crème de menthe (green peppermint liqueur)
8 egg whites
80g dark, bitter chocolate, chopped

CHOCOLATE PASTRY CREAM:
3 egg yolks
65g caster sugar
15g plain flour, sifted
1 tbsp cocoa powder
250ml milk

TO FINISH:
4 mint sprigs
icing sugar, to dust

Brush the insides of 4 individual 10cm soufflé dishes (6cm deep) with the softened butter. Put the 30g caster sugar into one dish and rotate it to coat the surface completely with sugar. Tip the excess sugar into the next dish and repeat until all the dishes are coated.

To make the pastry cream, whisk the egg yolks with one-third of the sugar in a bowl until pale, smooth and thick enough to leave a light ribbon trail when the whisk is lifted. Whisk in the flour and cocoa powder thoroughly. In a saucepan, bring the milk to the boil with the remaining sugar. As soon as it begins to bubble, pour about one-third onto the egg mixture, stirring continuously. Pour this custard back into the pan and bring to the boil over a gentle heat, stirring continuously. Let bubble for 2 minutes, then transfer to a bowl. Dust the surface lightly with icing sugar to prevent a skin forming and cool until tepid.

Preheat the oven to 190°C/Gas 5 and put a baking sheet inside to heat. Measure 300g of the just-warm pastry cream, place in a large bowl and stir in the peppermint liqueur.

Beat the egg whites in a clean bowl until half-risen, then add the 150g caster sugar and beat to semi-firm peaks. Use a whisk to mix one-third of the beaten egg whites into the pastry cream, then delicately fold in the rest with a spatula. Scatter in the chocolate.

Pour the mixture into the prepared soufflé dishes and smooth the surface with a palette knife. Use the tip of a knife to ease the mixture away from the edge of the dishes. Place the soufflé dishes on the hot baking sheet and cook in the hot oven for 7–8 minutes.

As soon as the soufflés come out of the oven, top each one with a mint sprig and dust with a light veil of icing sugar. Place each dish on a plate and serve immediately.

Mrs Beeton's
Chocolate Soufflé

SERVES 4

butter, to grease
4 large eggs, separated
3 heaped tsp caster sugar

1 heaped tsp plain flour
75g dark chocolate, grated
icing sugar, to dust

Preheat the oven to 190°C/Gas 5. Butter a 750ml soufflé dish. Beat the egg yolks, sugar, flour and chocolate together in a bowl for about 5 minutes.

Whisk the egg whites in a clean bowl until firm, then gently fold into the mixture until evenly incorporated. Pour into the prepared dish and bake for 15–20 minutes until well risen.

Sprinkle with icing sugar and serve immediately – take straight from the oven to the table before the soufflé has a chance to fall. A jug of pouring cream on the side won't go amiss.

A splendid pudding –
richly flavoured and easy to make!

A magical recipe – the sauce is poured over the sponge mixture, yet after baking the rich, dark sauce is hidden beneath the chocolate sponge.

Sarah Edington's
Chocolate Fudge Pudding

SERVES 4

110g butter, plus extra to grease
110g caster sugar
2 eggs
175g self-raising flour
2 tbsp cocoa powder
a little milk, if necessary

SAUCE:
300ml water
75g soft brown sugar
3 tbsp cocoa powder

Preheat the oven to 180°C/Gas 4. Butter an ovenproof oval dish, approximately 20 x 23cm and 10cm deep.

Cream the butter and sugar together in a bowl until pale and fluffy. Beat in the eggs, one at a time, adding a spoonful of flour with each one. Sift the remaining flour and cocoa powder together over the mixture and fold in carefully, adding a little milk if the mixture seems too stiff. Spread the mixture in the prepared dish.

For the sauce, gently heat the water, brown sugar and cocoa in a saucepan until the sugar is dissolved and you have a thinnish sauce.

Pour the sauce over the pudding mixture and bake in the oven for 45–55 minutes, until it is crisp and brown on top. Serve warm, with pouring cream.

Henrietta Green's
Chocolate Puddings
with orange cream

SERVES 6

200g butter, plus extra to grease
3 tsp plain flour, sifted, plus extra
   to dust
200g dark, bitter chocolate, in
   pieces
3 medium eggs, plus 3 egg yolks
6 tbsp caster sugar

ORANGE CREAM:
250g crème fraîche
50g icing sugar, sifted
grated zest and juice of 1 orange

TO FINISH:
25g dark chocolate, grated

Preheat the oven to 220°C/Gas 7. Lightly butter six 125ml ramekins
and dust very lightly with flour.

Melt the chocolate and butter in a heatproof bowl set over a pan
of simmering water (or in a microwave). Take off the heat, stir well
and leave to cool slightly.

In a separate bowl, whisk the eggs, egg yolks and sugar together
until thick and pale in colour. Whisk in the melted chocolate
mixture and then gently fold in the flour.

Pour the mixture into the prepared ramekins. (You can prepare the
puddings ahead to this stage; keep in the fridge and bring back to
room temperature before baking).

Stand the ramekins on a baking tray and bake in the oven for
about 6 minutes until set, but still soft and runny in the centre.

Meanwhile, to make the orange cream, put the crème fraîche into a
bowl, stir in the icing sugar, then gradually stir in the orange zest
and juice.

As soon as the puddings are ready, turn out each one onto a plate,
gently lifting off the ramekin. Top with a spoonful of orange
cream, sprinkle with grated chocolate and serve immediately.

Gloriously indulgent
puddings that will be made or marred by
the quality of the ingredients you use.
A really good dark chocolate with a high
cocoa solid content is imperative.

Dark, rich and gooey … these brownies are divine. For total decadence, top with the ganache – it's up to you!

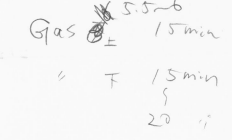

Gas ~~6~~ 5.5~6 15 min
~~↓~~ F 15 min
20

Bea Harling's
Gooey Chocolate Browni

MAKES 12

125g butter
150g dark chocolate, in pieces
175g soft dark brown sugar
2 large eggs
1 tsp vanilla extract
55g plain flour
1 tsp baking powder

GANACHE (OPTIONAL):
125g dark chocolate, in pie
small knob of butter
150ml whipping cream

Preheat the oven to 180°C/Gas 4. Line an 18cm square bakin
with baking parchment. Melt the butter with 50g of the chocolate
in a heatproof bowl set over a pan of gently simmering water.
Chop the remaining chocolate into rough chunks and set aside.

In a large bowl, beat the brown sugar with the eggs and vanilla
extract. Mix in the flour and baking powder, then stir in the melted
chocolate mixture. Finally add the chocolate chunks, stirring until
evenly combined. Pour the mixture into the tin.

Bake in the oven for about 30 minutes until the brownie begins to
shrink from the sides of the tin and is just firm on top. It should still
be soft and a little gooey in the middle. Leave in the tin for 5 minutes,
then transfer to a wire rack to cool. Cut into squares.

To make the ganache, if required, warm the chocolate with the
butter and cream in a heavy-based pan over a low heat to just below
boiling point. Stir until smooth, then take off the heat and allow to
cool slightly. Pour the ganache on top of the brownies and serve.

Frank Bordoni's
Budino di Cioccolata

SERVES 6
vegetable oil, to grease
350g dark chocolate, in pieces
60g unsalted butter, softened
150g caster sugar
4 large eggs, beaten
1 tsp vanilla extract
50g plain flour, sifted

Preheat the oven to 200°C/Gas 6 and place a baking sheet inside to heat up. Line the base of six individual pudding moulds with a disc of greaseproof paper and oil well.

Melt the chocolate (see page 13), take off the heat and set aside.

In a large bowl, cream together the butter and sugar until pale and fluffy. Gradually beat in the eggs and vanilla extract. Now add the flour and blend in the chocolate to make a smooth batter.

Divide the mixture evenly between the prepared moulds. Stand them on the hot baking sheet and bake in the oven for 10 minutes until well risen.

Immediately turn out the puddings onto warm plates. Serve straight away with a dollop of mascarpone or pouring cream.

Oozing, moist rich centres make these puddings wickedly indulgent. Serve them with mascarpone flavoured with a little vanilla.

Mary Cadogan's
Dark Mocha Soufflés

SERVES 6

butter, to grease
1 tbsp ground almonds, to dust
150g dark chocolate, in pieces
4 tbsp strong black coffee, cooled
4 eggs, separated
2 tsp plain flour
100g caster sugar

MOCHA SAUCE:
100g dark chocolate, in pieces
150ml double cream
2 tbsp strong black coffee, cooled
2 tbsp brandy

TO SERVE:
luxury vanilla ice cream

Preheat the oven to 190°C/Gas 5. Generously butter six 200ml ramekins or ovenproof teacups and dust the insides lightly with the ground almonds.

Put the chocolate and coffee in a bowl over a pan of simmering water and stir gently until melted. Remove from the heat and leave to cool for a few minutes, then stir in the egg yolks, flour and half the sugar.

Whisk the egg whites in a clean bowl until firm, then whisk in the remaining sugar, a tablespoonful at a time. Fold a quarter of the egg white into the chocolate mixture, then carefully fold in the remainder, using a metal spoon, until evenly blended.

Divide the mixture among the prepared dishes and bake in the oven for 20–25 minutes until well risen.

Meanwhile, for the sauce, put the chocolate, cream and coffee in a pan and stir over a very low heat until melted, smooth and shiny. Stir in the brandy and pour into a jug.

Serve the soufflés the moment they are ready. Each diner splits open their soufflé, adds a scoop of ice cream and pours over some chocolate sauce.

With a brandy kick
and the punch of strong coffee, these mouth-watering soufflés are the perfect way to round off a dinner party.

Fran Warde's
Tarte Belle Helene

SERVES 10

PÂTE SUCRÉE:

60g butter, diced, plus extra to
grease
140g plain flour
50g icing sugar, sifted, plus extra
to dust
2 medium egg yolks, lightly
whisked

FILLING:

3 firm, ripe pears
55g butter
75g golden caster or light
muscovado sugar
1 egg
20g ground almonds
75g self-raising flour
¼ tsp baking powder
25g cocoa powder
50ml milk

Preheat the oven to 190°C/gas 5. Lightly butter a 25cm flan ring
and place it on a buttered baking sheet.

To make the pastry, sift the flour into a large bowl, add the butter
and rub together with your fingertips until the texture resembles
breadcrumbs. Now add the icing sugar and mix through. Add
two-thirds of the egg yolks and mix to combine, using a round-
bladed knife in a cutting motion until the mixture forms a ball
(adding the remaining egg if necessary). Wrap in cling film and chill
in the fridge for 30 minutes.

Lightly dust a cool surface with icing sugar and roll out the pastry
to a 25cm circle, to just fit inside the flan ring. Carefully drape the
pastry over the rolling pin and unroll it into the flan ring on the
baking sheet. Using your fingers, mould the pastry into the ring to
form the base of the tart, then chill for a further 30 minutes.

For the filling, peel, halve and core the pears and arrange cut-side
down on the pastry base. Cream the butter and sugar together in a
bowl. Add the egg and beat in, then mix in the ground almonds.
Sift the flour, baking powder and cocoa together, and fold into the
mixture with the milk. Spoon onto the pastry base around the
pears and smooth the top.

Bake in the oven for 30 minutes, then cover the top loosely with
foil and bake for a further 15 minutes. Dust the tart with a little
icing sugar before serving.

Pears and chocolate
have always been something of a winning
combination. Serve this tart just warm,
with vanilla ice cream. The pastry is delicate,
crumbly and sweet.

Ed Baines'
Chocolate Ricotta Tart

SERVES 10–12

PASTA FROLLA:
225g plain flour, plus extra
    to dust
pinch of salt
100g unsalted butter, diced
30g caster sugar
1 egg, beaten
3 tbsp cold water

FILLING:
350g ricotta cheese
85g caster sugar

3 eggs
grated zest and juice of 1 lemon
grated zest and juice of ½ orange
60g blanched almonds, finely
    chopped
60g finely chopped mixed peel
4 drops of vanilla extract
100g dark chocolate, grated

TO FINISH:
chocolate ganache (see page 15),
    or icing sugar, to dust

To make the pastry, put the flour, salt and butter in a large bowl and rub through with your fingers until the mixture is the consistency of breadcrumbs. Mix in the sugar, then the egg, together with the cold water to make a smooth dough. Knead lightly and gently to ensure a light crumbly pastry. Form the pastry into a ball, wrap in cling film and chill in the fridge for 30 minutes.

Meanwhile, make the filling. Put the ricotta in a sieve to drain off any excess water, then tip into a bowl. Gradually beat in the sugar and the eggs, using a wooden spoon. Stir in the citrus zests and juices. Now mix in the almonds and chopped peel, then the vanilla extract and finally the grated chocolate. Cover and chill.

Preheat the oven to 180°C/Gas 4. Roll out the pastry on a well-floured surface and use it to line a 25cm tart tin. Cut away the excess pastry, overhanging the rim.

Pour the ricotta filling into the pastry case and smooth evenly. Bake in the oven for 45–50 minutes, until light golden brown on top. Allow to cool.

Decorate the tart with curls of chocolate ganache or dust with icing sugar to serve.

Lavishly topped with curls of chocolate ganache, this tart looks stunning, but for a simple finish you can simply dust it with icing sugar. The pastry, known as *pasta frolla*, is deliciously crumbly and worth making, but if you really haven't the time, you could use a packet of ready-made sweet pastry instead.

Terry Laybourne's
Profiteroles
with hot chocolate sauce

SERVES 6

CHOUX PASTRY:
125ml water
125ml milk
½ tsp salt
½ tsp sugar
100g unsalted butter
150g strong plain flour, sifted
4 eggs, beaten

CHOCOLATE SAUCE:
100g dark chocolate
75ml milk
1 tbsp double cream
1 tbsp sugar
1 tbsp softened butter

FILLING:
500ml vanilla or pistachio ice
    cream

To make the choux pastry, put the water, milk, salt, sugar and butter into a medium saucepan. Bring to the boil, take off the heat and immediately add all the flour in one go, stirring well. Return to the heat and beat vigorously until smooth. Continue cooking over a medium heat for a minute or two until the paste leaves the sides of the pan. Remove from the heat and allow to cool for 3 minutes.

Weigh 200g of the beaten eggs. Begin adding the egg to the mixture a little at a time, beating well between each addition. Once it is all incorporated, the choux pastry should be smooth, shiny and thick enough to pipe.

Preheat the oven to 200°C/Gas 6. Grease a large baking tray. Put the choux pastry into a piping bag fitted with a 12mm plain nozzle. Pipe 18 small mounds onto the baking tray, spacing them well apart. Bake for 10 minutes, then lower the heat to 140°C/Gas 1 and bake for a further 20 minutes. Transfer to a wire rack to cool.

For the sauce, melt the chocolate (see page 13). Put the milk, cream and sugar into a pan. Bring to the boil, then pour onto the melted chocolate, stirring well. Return to the pan and bring just back to the boil, then take off the heat and whisk in the butter. Keep warm.

To assemble, cut each choux bun in half and return to the oven for 3 minutes. Divide the choux bases between serving plates, allowing three per portion. Place a ball of ice cream on each base and top with the lids. Spoon the hot chocolate sauce over the profiteroles and serve immediately.

Crisp little choux buns filled with ice cream and topped with hot chocolate sauce – a classic, ever-popular dessert.

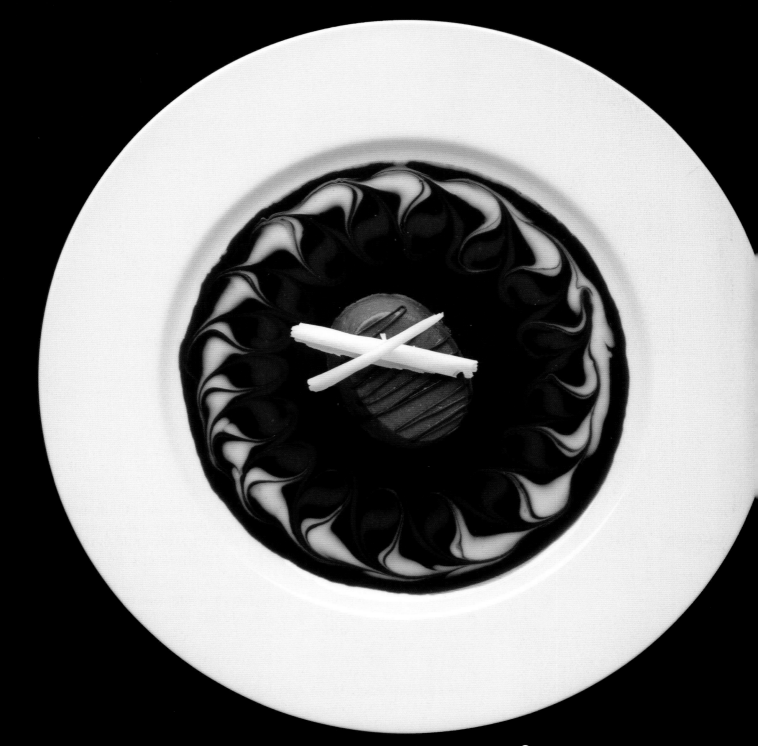

Anton Mosimann

Chocolate Mousse with White and Dark Chocolate Sauces

Elegant mousses –
smart enough for a special dinner
party dessert. It goes without saying
that you must use the finest chocolate.

SERVES 8
groundnut oil, to oil moulds
1 sheet of leaf gelatine
200g dark chocolate,
   in pieces
2 tbsp strong black coffee, cooled
2 tbsp Cognac
5 eggs, separated
90g caster sugar
150ml double cream

CHOCOLATE SAUCE:
225g dark chocolate, in pieces
75ml sugar syrup (see page 15)
150ml double cream

TO DECORATE:
50g milk chocolate, chopped
50g white chocolate, chopped
2 tbsp groundnut oil
white chocolate shavings
   (see page 15)

Oil 8 individual oval moulds or ramekins. Soak the gelatine in cold water to cover for a few minutes to soften. Put the chocolate, coffee and Cognac in a heatproof bowl and set over a pan of simmering water to melt the chocolate. Squeeze the gelatine to remove excess water, then add to the melted chocolate mixture and stir until dissolved. Take off the heat.

Whisk the egg yolks and 40g of the sugar together in a bowl until the sugar has dissolved. Stir the yolk mixture into the chocolate, taking care to ensure that the chocolate does not cool, or it will set before all the ingredients are added.

Whip the cream in a bowl until soft peaks form. In another bowl, whisk the egg whites with the remaining sugar to a 'snow'. Fold the whipped cream into the chocolate mixture, then fold in the whisked egg whites. Divide the mixture evenly among the moulds and smooth lightly. Cover and chill until set.

To make the chocolate sauce, melt the chocolate (see page 13), then take off the heat and stir in the sugar syrup. Pour the cream into a bowl and gradually blend in the chocolate mixture until you have a smooth sauce.

When ready to assemble the desserts, melt the milk chocolate and white chocolate separately over hot water (see page 13). Stir 1 tbsp groundnut oil into each melted chocolate until smooth and glossy.

Pour some of the dark chocolate sauce onto an individual serving plate, tapping the plate on the surface to spread it into a dark and shining circle. Unmould one mousse and place it in the middle. Pipe a circle of the white chocolate around the edge, then pipe a circle of milk chocolate within that. Spin a little dark chocolate sauce over the mousse. Marble the white and milk chocolate into the sauce decoratively, using a fine skewer.

Assemble the remaining desserts in the same way. Arrange a few white chocolate shavings on top of each mousse. Serve at once.

Tonia George's
Dark Chocolate Mousse

SERVES 4
150g dark chocolate (70% cocoa
**   solids), in pieces**
4 medium eggs, separated

Put the chocolate into a heatproof bowl and set over a pan of barely simmering water until half-melted. Take off the heat and beat until the last chunks liquefy. Set aside to cool, until lukewarm but still fluid. Meanwhile, in a large clean bowl, beat the egg whites with an electric or hand whisk until they form stiff peaks.

In a separate bowl, beat the egg yolks, add the melted chocolate and mix to combine. Fold in a third of the egg whites to loosen the mixture. Carefully fold in the rest of the whites, using a large metal spoon to lift the chocolate up through the whites, distributing it evenly. The lighter your folding, the lighter the mousse will be.

Divide the mousse among 4 ramekins or small serving cups and chill in the fridge for 1 hour before serving.

The perfect chocolate mousse needs only three things: fine quality chocolate, eggs at room temperature, and plenty of air. The secret is in the folding technique. You might like to vary the flavour – by adding a couple of drops of orange flower water or 1 tbsp chilli oil to the chocolate before melting it.

Rosemary Moon's
Milk Chocolate Mousse
flavoured with Earl Grey tea

SERVES 6

4 strong Earl Grey teabags
200g milk chocolate, in pieces
2 large eggs, separated
142ml carton double cream

TO FINISH:
whipped cream (optional)
milk chocolate, coarsely grated,
  to decorate

Put the tea bags in a measuring jug and add boiling water to the 100ml mark. Leave to infuse for 5 minutes, then remove the bags and leave the tea to cool slightly. Melt the chocolate (see page 13), beat until smooth, then leave to cool for a few minutes.

Whisk the egg whites in a clean bowl until stiff. Whip the cream in another bowl until thick and floppy.

Beat the egg yolks and the tea into the chocolate – as they combine the chocolate will become darker and glossy. Fold the cream into the chocolate with gentle figure-of-eight strokes. Finally incorporate the egg whites, half at a time, in the same way.

Spoon into small cups or serving dishes and chill for at least 2 hours. The tea flavour will continues to develop, so leave the mousses in the fridge for 6–8 hours before serving if possible.

To finish, pipe a swirl of whipped cream on top of each mousse if you like, and scatter with grated chocolate.

Earl Grey tea is a fabulous flavouring for chocolate, especially milk chocolate which works better than a more bitter, darker confection. Like any chocolate mousse, it is rich so the servings are small.

Lulu Grimes'
White Chocolate Creams

SERVES 4
250ml double cream
4 cardamom pods, lightly crushed
1 bay leaf
150g white chocolate
3 egg yolks

Put the cream, cardamom and bay leaf in a saucepan and slowly bring to the boil. Take off the heat and set aside to let the cardamom and bay leaf flavours infuse into the cream.

Grate or finely chop the white chocolate (to make it easier to melt) and put it into a bowl. Gently heat the cream up again until it is almost boiling and then strain through a sieve onto the chocolate. Stir until the chocolate has melted. Gently whisk the egg yolks in another bowl, then stir them into the chocolate mixture.

Pour the mixture into four espresso cups or very small bowls and place in the fridge to set. They should be ready in a couple of hours... if you don't keep opening the fridge door to look at them.

Smooth, rich little puddings that call for the best white chocolate you can find. The quality not only affects the flavour – if you use cheap chocolate the recipe may not work at all.

These exquisite little pots are ideal after a satisfying meal, when all you want is a few mouthfuls of sinful sweetness, without the bulk. Make them up to 8 hours in advance.

Celia Brooks Brown's
Strawberry Truffle Pots

SERVES 10

100g white chocolate
10 strawberries
10 silver sugar pearls (optional)
50g butter, cubed

250g dark chocolate
(minimum 70% cocoa solids),
in pieces
300ml double cream

Melt the white chocolate (see page 13). Take a slice off the hulled end of each strawberry to give a flat surface. Now, one at a time, hold by the hulled end and dip in the melted white chocolate, to coat halfway up the strawberry. Place hulled-side down on a plate. Press a silver sugar pearl into the chocolate at the very tip, if you like. Chill until the chocolate has set.

Stand 10 shot glasses or tiny bowls on a tray, ready to be filled. Put the butter, dark chocolate and cream in a pan over a very gentle heat and stir constantly until melted and very smooth, then remove from the heat. Divide the truffle mixture among the shot glasses or bowls. Chill until set, about 30 minutes.

Place a chocolate-dipped strawberry on top of each truffle serving. Return to room temperature before serving.

Antony Worrall Thompson's
Chocolate Parfait
with Summer Berries

SERVES 4–6

grapeseed or sunflower oil, to grease
85g dark chocolate (minimum 70% cocoa solids), in pieces
40g unsalted butter
5 tbsp caster sugar
2 eggs, separated
1 tbsp brandy
3 tbsp cocoa powder

175g fresh cherries, pitted and chopped
150ml double cream

TO SERVE:
225g mixed berries, such as blueberries, strawberries and raspberries
raspberry sauce, see note (optional)

Line a 450g loaf tin with oiled cling film. Melt the chocolate with half of the butter in a heatproof bowl set over a pan of simmering water. Take off the heat and leave to cool slightly.

Using a hand-held electric beater, beat the rest of the butter with 2 tbsp of the sugar in a large bowl until light and fluffy. Gradually beat in the egg yolks, brandy and cocoa powder, adding a little cocoa after each addition of egg yolk to stop the mixture from splitting. Fold in the cooled melted chocolate mixture, together with the chopped cherries.

Whip the cream in a bowl to soft peaks. Whisk the egg whites in a separate bowl until softly peaking, then add the remaining sugar and whisk until stiff and glossy. Fold the cream into the chocolate mixture, then gently fold in the egg whites until just combined.

Carefully pour the chocolate mixture into the prepared loaf tin and cover with cling film. Freeze for at least 4 hours until solid, but preferably overnight.

Remove the parfait from the freezer about 20 minutes before you are ready to serve. Turn out onto a board and carefully peel away the cling film. Cut into slices and arrange on individual plates with the summer berries and a dribble of raspberry sauce, if you like.

I serve this parfait with a scattering of berries and a drizzle of raspberry sauce. You can buy good quality ready-made raspberry sauce, but it's easy to make your own. Purée a punnet of raspberries in a food processor or blender with a squeeze of lemon juice and icing sugar to taste, then pass through a sieve to remove the seeds.

Linda Tubby's
Chocolate Prune Galettes

SERVES 6
150g dark chocolate, in pieces
200g ready-to-eat pitted prunes
2 tbsp Armagnac
500ml double cream
2 tbsp icing sugar, plus extra
   to dust
24 crystallised violets, to decorate
   (optional)

Line a board or a large baking sheet with greaseproof paper. Melt the chocolate (see page 13), stir until smooth, then spread evenly over the paper to a rough shape about 28cm x 35cm, using a palette knife. Set aside in a cool place to harden.

When firm, cut the chocolate into 18 rectangular shapes, using a long sharp knife (heated in boiling water and dried before cutting). Store the chocolate shapes interleaved with greaseproof paper in an airtight container in a cool place until required. (They can be made up to 2 days in advance.)

Finely chop the prunes and soak in the Armagnac for 10 minutes. Purée the prunes and liquor in a food processor as finely as possible, then add 150ml of the cream and whiz briefly to combine. Pass the mixture through a sieve into a bowl, pressing it through with a wooden spoon.

Stir another 50ml cream into the creamy prune purée to loosen it. Add the remaining cream and icing sugar and stir with a wooden spoon until just thick enough to pipe. Transfer the mixture to a piping bag fitted with a 1.5cm fluted nozzle.

Lay 12 chocolate rectangles out on a surface and pipe a whirl of prune cream on top of each one. Stack them in pairs, then top with another chocolate rectangle, making 6 stacks in total. Transfer to individual serving plates, using a palette knife.

Cut some strips of paper, about 7mm wide and as long as necessary to cover a chocolate rectangle. Lay across the top of each stack diagonally in parallel and sift over the icing sugar. Carefully lift off the paper, leaving decorative bands. Decorate with crystallised violets if you like.

An exquisite dessert that is deceptively simple and quick to prepare. Be as neat or as casual as you like in constructing the 'galettes' – the chocolate shapes and icing sugar finish needn't be precise.

Mark Hix's
Iced Berries
with hot white chocolate sauce

SERVES 8
1kg mixed frozen small-medium
   berries, or just raspberries
   (see note)

SAUCE:
600g good quality white
   chocolate buttons
600ml double cream

Simple and irresistible –
probably more so than any other pudding
you'll make – a dinner-party classic. Either
buy a bag of mixed frozen berries or
raspberries, or freeze your own selection.
Larger berries, such as strawberries and big
blackberries, are not recommended, as they
don't defrost quickly enough.

To make the sauce, put the white chocolate and cream into a heatproof bowl set over a pan of gently simmering water for 20–30 minutes, stirring every so often, until the chocolate has melted and the sauce is hot. Stir until smooth.

Five minutes before serving, divide the berries among dessert plates and leave at room temperature, so they lose a little of their chill. Transfer the chocolate sauce to a warm serving jug.

Place the berries in front of your guests and pour on the hot chocolate sauce at the table, covering the berries generously.

Better than ice cream

— this is a rich, creamy, gooey, moussey parfait, that's ready to slice, chop or scoop. Use a light hand to fold the cream into the chocolate mixture — it's preferable to have a few streaks of cream through the mousse than lose all the lightness and volume.

Jill Dupleix's
Frozen Chocolate Mousse

SERVES 6

200g dark, bittersweet chocolate,
   chopped
2 large eggs, plus 2 egg yolks
100g caster sugar
1 tsp vanilla extract

2 tbsp whisky, Cognac or
   Amaretto liqueur
250ml whipping cream
cocoa powder, to dust

Melt the chocolate in a heatproof bowl set over a pan of gently simmering water, then set aside to cool for 3 minutes.

In a bowl, beat the eggs, egg yolks and sugar together for a few minutes, using a hand-held electric beater, until pale and thick. Add the melted chocolate and beat constantly for about 3 minutes, then stir in the vanilla extract and whisky.

In another bowl, whip the cream until it forms light peaks. Fold the cream lightly through the chocolate mixture, then pour into a 1 litre loaf tin. Cover with cling film and freeze overnight.

To serve, soften the mousse in the refrigerator for 15 minutes, or dip the base of the tin very briefly in hot water and run a knife around the edges. Turn out and cut into thick slices or chunks, or scoop straight from the tin. Serve immediately, dusted with cocoa powder.

Robin Weir's
Ultimate Chocolate Ice Cream

MAKES 875ml

5 tbsp cocoa powder
90g granulated sugar
375ml full-fat milk
150g dark chocolate (about 70% cocoa solids), finely chopped

65ml sugar syrup (see recipe)
3 egg yolks
1 tsp vanilla extract
1 tsp instant coffee granules
250ml whipping cream

Combine the cocoa powder and half the sugar in a small bowl. Mix in enough of the milk to form a thin paste. Bring the rest of the milk to the boil in a heavy-based pan. Pour the hot milk onto the blended cocoa, whisking constantly, then return the mixture to the pan. Return to a very low heat (or position the pan on a heat-diffuser mat) and heat slowly to simmering point, stirring constantly.

Now continue to cook gently, stirring, for 6 minutes. This stage is very important, as the long slow cooking ensures all the powdery flavour of the cocoa is cooked out. So take it slowly, and keep stirring, because the cocoa blend will catch on the base of the pan the moment your attention wanders. Remove the pan from the heat and stir in the chopped chocolate.

For the sugar syrup, dissolve 50g sugar in 50ml water in a pan over a low heat, then bring to the boil. Allow to cool, then measure 65ml for the ice cream and chill.

Beat the egg yolks and remaining sugar together in a bowl until pale. Pour in the chocolate mixture, beating vigorously, then immediately return to the pan. Again, with the saucepan on a very low heat or heat-diffuser mat, heat slowly, stirring until the temperature registers 85°C on a cooking thermometer.

Remove from the heat and stir in the vanilla extract, coffee granules and sugar syrup. Sit the base of the pan in cold water to hasten cooling and leave until cold. Strain the mixture into a bowl (there will be bits in it), then cover and chill in the fridge.

Beat the cream into the chilled chocolate mixture. Now churn in an ice-cream machine according to the manufacturer's instructions until the ice cream is the consistency of whipped cream, about 20 minutes. Quickly scrape into freezerproof plastic containers and level the surface. Cover with greaseproof paper and a lid, then freeze.

Ideally, the ice cream should be eaten within 2 hours. If frozen solid, soften for about 20 minutes in the fridge before serving. Scoop into dishes and serve on its own. Enjoy the experience...

Bertillon, on the Ile de la Cité in Paris, make the best commercially produced chocolate ice cream I've ever tasted. This started a quest to come up with the ultimate chocolate ice cream recipe... and this is it.

This gâteau is to die for, and once mastered, is relatively simple and quick to make. However, you do need to follow the instructions carefully. Reducing the quantities doesn't really work but the gâteau keeps for at least 7 days in the fridge – and freezes like a dream. It's great with all sorts of fruit, custard and ice cream.

Sara Jayne Stanes
Truffe Gâteau

SERVES 12–15
450g dark chocolate
500ml whipping cream, at room
   temperature
3 tbsp rum (optional)

To Finish:
cocoa powder or icing sugar,
   to dust
pinch of ground cinnamon
   (optional)

Line a 25.5cm flan ring placed on a tray, or an oblong container, about 21cm x 7.5cm x 10cm deep, with cling film. Melt the chocolate slowly in a heatproof bowl over a pan of hot water (don't let the water temperature rise above 40°C).

Meanwhile, lightly whip the cream, and rum if using, in a large bowl until the whisk leaves a soft trail. The melted chocolate must be at about 35°C. Pour about half of it into the cream and fold in. Then fold in the rest of the chocolate until totally amalgamated.

Pour the mixture into the prepared ring or container and gently smooth the top. Chill for at least 3 hours or longer for a really firm finish. Turn out and dust with cocoa powder or icing sugar mixed with a touch of cinnamon if you like (not too much or it will be overpowering). Serve cut into thin slices.

Ice cream wafers were something I enjoyed as a kid, although at that age I was oblivious to the dodgy quality. This is a kind of cross between a choc ice and one of those ice cream wafers. It makes a fun dessert for kids and grown-ups and you can keep the wafers handy in the freezer as a snack.

MAKES 8–10
450ml milk
6 egg yolks
150g caster sugar
400ml Jersey or clotted cream, or a mixture
a couple of handfuls of mint leaves
600g dark chocolate

Pour the milk into a heavy-based saucepan and bring just to the boil, then remove from the heat. Whisk the egg yolks and sugar together in a bowl, then pour on the milk, whisking well. Return to the pan and stir constantly with a whisk over a low heat for about 5 minutes, but don't let it boil.

Pour the custard into a bowl, whisk in the cream and leave to cool. Pour four-fifths of the mixture into an ice cream machine and churn according to the manufacturer's instructions.

Meanwhile, bring a small pan of water to the boil and blanch the mint leaves for 15 seconds, then drain and refresh under cold running water. Squeeze out any excess water, then whiz the leaves in a blender with the remaining cream-custard mixture.

Line a 2–3cm deep freezerproof tray with cling film or greaseproof paper When the ice cream is beginning to freeze, add the mint mixture and continue churning. Chop half the chocolate into small pieces, add to the ice cream machine and churn for a minute or two. Transfer the ice cream to the prepared tray, cover with cling film and place in the freezer for a couple of hours or until the mixture is firm.

Meanwhile, melt the rest of the chocolate in a bowl over a pan of simmering water. Line a tray with greaseproof or silicone paper. Pour the chocolate onto it and spread to a 4–5mm thickness. Leave to set.

When the ice cream is firm, cut it into squares or rectangles and return to the freezer. Dip a knife into boiling water, dry it with a tea-towel and cut the chocolate into the same sized pieces as the ice cream. Sandwich the ice cream between the chocolate shapes and return to the freezer until required.

Mark Hix's
Mint Choc Chip Sandwich

Lyn Hall's
Cocoa-dusted Truffle Cake

SERVES 8–10

1 chocolate sponge cake, trimmed
   to an 18cm square, 5mm thick
25g sugar
50ml water
100ml raspberry liqueur or
   Cognac

220g dark chocolate, chopped
500ml whipping cream
cocoa powder, to dust
raspberries, to finish (optional)

Line the base of a 10cm deep, 18cm square or 20cm round cake tin with a piece of thick card cut to fit. Press the sponge onto the card to fit exactly. Dissolve the sugar in the water in a pan over a low heat, then bring to the boil; let cool. Mix the sugar syrup with the alcohol and dab over the sponge evenly with a pastry brush.

Melt the chocolate (see page 13). Whip the cream until starting to peak. Still whisking, pour on the hot melted chocolate, whisking to amalgamate evenly. Immediately pour over the sponge base in the prepared tin and leave to set. Chill overnight if possible.

Carefully remove the cake from the tin. Dust with cocoa and top with raspberries if wished. Cut into portions with a warm knife.

This tempting truffle cake is quick and easy to make, using a ready-made sponge. If possible, prepare a day ahead and chill overnight to let the flavours develop.

Mary Berry's
White Chocolate Cheesecake
with summer berries

SERVES 8–10

BASE:
50g butter, plus extra to grease
150g plain chocolate digestive
    biscuits, crushed

FILLING:
300g white chocolate, in pieces
400g full-fat cream cheese

2 eggs
150ml soured cream
1 tsp vanilla extract

TO SERVE:
cocoa powder, to dust
about 225g strawberries or
    raspberries

Preheat the oven to 160°C/Gas 3. Grease a deep 20cm springform cake tin and line the base with baking parchment.

Melt the butter in a pan over a low heat. Stir in the crushed biscuits and press evenly over the base of the prepared tin. Chill in the fridge to firm up.

Melt the white chocolate (see page 13), stirring occasionally with a spoon until runny and smooth. Allow to cool slightly.

Whisk the cream cheese and eggs together in a large bowl until smooth, then add the soured cream and vanilla extract and whisk again until the mixture is completely smooth. Stir in the melted chocolate until evenly combined.

Pour this mixture over the biscuit base in the tin and spread evenly. Bake in the oven for about 45 minutes until firm around the edge and just set in the middle. As you remove it from the oven, run a small palette knife around the edge of the cheesecake, and then leave to cool in the tin. The surface may crack slightly in the middle, but don't worry, this is part of its charm! Once cool, chill.

To serve, release the tin and remove the side, leaving the cheesecake on the base. Dust with cocoa powder and cut into slices. Serve topped with strawberries or raspberries.

This cheesecake is very rich, but so delicious! You can make it a day ahead for convenience.

Paul and Jeanne Rankin's
Chocolate Espresso Cake

SERVES 8–10

BASE AND TOPPING:
175g hazelnuts, toasted and
  skinned
125g butter, diced
25g soft light brown sugar
40g caster sugar
125g plain flour
1½ tbsp cornflour
pinch of salt

FILLING:
400ml double cream
100ml single cream
300g dark chocolate, finely
  chopped

100g milk chocolate, finely
  chopped
2 eggs
1 tsp vanilla extract
1 tsp coffee extract (or very
  strong black coffee)

COFFEE CREAM:
½ leaf gelatine or 1 scant tsp
  powdered gelatine
250ml whipping cream
4 tbsp icing sugar
3½ tbsp coffee extract (or very
  strong black coffee)

Preheat the oven to 170°C/Gas 3. Have ready a 23cm springform cake tin. Whiz the hazelnuts in a food processor until roughly chopped. Tip half of them into a bowl and reserve for the topping.

For the base, add the butter, sugars, flour, cornflour and salt to the hazelnuts in the processor and process briefly to a crumbly texture. Tip into the cake tin and pat onto the base in an even layer. Bake for 15–20 minutes until golden brown, but no darker. Remove and set aside to cool. Reduce the oven setting to 160°C/ Gas mark 2½.

For the filling, pour both creams into a pan and bring to the boil, then remove from the heat and cool slightly. Add the dark and milk chocolate and stir until melted, then stir in the eggs, vanilla and coffee extracts.

Pour the filling over the base and bake on the centre shelf of the oven for 15–20 minutes until just set but still slightly wobbly in the centre. Leave to cool.

To make the coffee cream, soften the gelatine in 2 tbsp cold water for a few minutes, then heat gently to dissolve and set aside to cool slightly. Whip the cream until it forms soft peaks, sift in the icing sugar and fold in the dissolved gelatine and coffee extract. Spread in an even layer over the chocolate filling and leave to set.

When ready to serve, scatter the reserved hazelnuts on top. Serve cut into slices, with chocolate sauce (see page 15) and lightly whipped cream if you're feeling totally indulgent.

A dark, sumptuous cake of smooth chocolate and coffee-flavoured cream stacked on a biscuit and hazelnut base, finished with a topping of crunchy toasted hazelnuts.

Like a chocolate mousse that has been baked to form a crust, this is incredibly rich, so serve it simply with crème fraîche or whipped cream.

Peter Gordon's
Chocolate Mousse Cake
with star anise

10–12 SLICES

300g dark chocolate (minimum 60% cocoa solids), in pieces
150g unsalted butter
6 eggs, separated

1½ tsp freshly ground star anise, sifted
50g caster sugar

Preheat the oven to 180°C/Gas 4. Line the base and sides of a 20cm springform cake tin with greaseproof paper. Melt the chocolate and butter in a heatproof bowl set over a pan of simmering water, stir until smooth, then let cool slightly.

Whisk the egg yolks with the star anise and 2 tbsp sugar for 30 seconds or so, then add the melted chocolate and mix well.

In a clean bowl, whisk the egg whites until stiff, then gradually whisk in the remaining sugar until very stiff. Quickly fold one-third into the chocolate mix to loosen it, then gently fold in the rest. Pour the mixture into the prepared tin.

Bake on the middle shelf of the oven for about 20 minutes. As you take it out, cover the tin with foil, sealing well to keep in the steam as this will soften the crust. Once cold, chill for at least 4 hours.

Serve the mousse cake cut into wedges, with a dollop of crème fraîche or whipped cream.

Jane Suthering's
Chocolate Mud Pie

SERVES 10–12

PASTRY:

125g plain flour
15g cocoa powder
40g icing sugar
75g unsalted butter
1 egg yolk

FILLING:

175g dark chocolate
175g unsalted butter
175g light or dark muscovado
  sugar
2 tsp instant coffee powder
3 eggs, plus 1 egg white
142ml carton whipping cream
100g pecan nuts, roughly
  chopped

Whiz all the ingredients for the pastry in a food processor to make a firm dough. Roll out thinly and use to line a 25cm fluted flan tin – use all the pastry and don't worry if you have to patch it! Chill in the fridge for 20 minutes. Preheat the oven to 190°C/Gas 5.

Line the pastry case with greaseproof paper and baking beans and bake blind for 15 minutes. Remove the beans and paper and cook for a further 10 minutes.

Meanwhile, for the filling, slowly melt the chocolate and butter in a pan over a very low heat. Take off the heat and beat in the remaining ingredients.

Pour the filling into the pastry case and bake for about 25 minutes until lightly risen and just firm. Leave to go cold before serving, sliced into wedges.

More enticing than its name suggests, this dark tart has a gorgeous rich chocolate and pecan nut filling.

A heavenly, rich dessert that relies on the use of top quality dark chocolate. To enjoy it at its best, serve it at room temperature. For a special occasion, decorate with a simple flower arrangement.

Grace Mulligan's
Rich Mousse Cake

SERVES 8–10

SPONGE:
3 extra large eggs
75g caster sugar
75g plain flour, less 1 heaped tsp
1 heaped tsp cocoa powder

CHOCOLATE MOUSSE:
5 sheets of leaf gelatine
    (measuring 12 x 7.5cm)
6 tbsp water
175g dark chocolate, in pieces
2 tsp instant coffee granules
4 extra large eggs, separated
50g caster sugar
140ml whipping cream

TO DECORATE:
white chocolate buttons and dark
    chocolate shapes, or icing sugar
    to dust

For the sponge, preheat the oven to 140°C/Gas 1. Grease a 20cm springform cake tin (at least 7.5cm deep) and line the base with greaseproof paper.

Using an electric mixer (or hand-held electric beater), whisk the eggs and sugar together until very thick. Sift about one-third of the flour and cocoa powder over the egg mixture, then using a spatula and a figure-of-eight movement, lightly fold the two together. Repeat twice more to incorporate the rest of the flour and cocoa, taking care to cut through the mixture with the sharp edge of the spatula only. Try to keep the mixture as fluffy as possible.

Pour the mixture into the cake tin and bake in the middle of the oven for 30–40 minutes or until the sponge has risen, is firm on top and beginning to shrink from the sides of the tin. Allow to cool in the tin for about 10 minutes, then run a thin knife round the sponge. Turn out onto the palm of your hand, peel off the paper and set on a wire rack to cool completely.

For the chocolate mousse, cut the gelatine into small pieces, using scissors. Put these in a small bowl with 3 tbsp water and leave to soften for a few minutes, then stand the bowl over a pan of gently simmering water until the gelatine dissolves, leaving a clear liquid.

Melt the chocolate with the coffee and 3 tbsp water in a heatproof bowl over a pan of gently simmering water, stirring a few times until smooth. Stir in the gelatine and remove from the heat.

In another bowl, whisk the egg yolks and sugar together until very thick, then fold into the chocolate mixture. Set aside to cool. Whip the cream until thick and fold into the mixture. Now whisk the egg whites in a clean bowl until soft peaks form. Carefully fold into the mixture. Set aside until beginning to set.

Now assemble the dessert. Slice the chocolate sponge horizontally into two layers and place one half on a large flat plate. Ease the ring of your springform tin (without its base) over the sponge layer so it fits snugly around the sponge base. Pour the chocolate mousse on top of the sponge and place in the fridge to set. (Freeze the other sponge round to use for another dessert.)

To serve, run a knife round the mousse and release the springform ring. Decorate with white chocolate buttons and dark chocolate shapes, or just a dusting of icing sugar at the last minute.

Linda Collister's
White Chocolate Cheesecake
with rhubarb

Grease a 24cm springform cake tin. Preheat the oven to 150°C/Gas 2.

To make the crust, mix the crushed biscuits with the sugar and melted butter. Tip into the prepared tin and press onto the base with the back of a spoon, to form an even layer. Chill.

To make the filling, melt the white chocolate (see page 13) and let cool slightly. Using an electric mixer (or hand-held electric beater) on a low speed, beat the cream cheese, lemon zest, vanilla extract and sugar together until the mixture is very smooth. Increase the speed and gradually beat in the eggs, scraping down the sides from time to time, until evenly combined. Pour in the soured cream and mix thoroughly. Finally mix in the melted chocolate.

Pour the filling over the biscuit base in the tin (it will be almost full). Set the tin on a baking tray and bake in the oven for 1¾ hours or until almost firm. Turn off the oven and leave the cheesecake inside to cool slowly. (The cheesecake will puff up on baking, then sink down and usually crack on cooling.)

After it has been cooling for an hour, set the oven door ajar. Leave the cheesecake inside until completely cold, then remove, cover and chill overnight.

For the topping, heat the oven to 180°C/Gas 4. Cut the rhubarb into 3cm pieces. Spread the redcurrant jelly over the base of a baking dish and arrange the rhubarb in a single layer on top. Cover and cook gently in the oven for 20 minutes or until just tender. Leave to cool.

When ready to finish the cheesecake, remove the rhubarb from the liquor with a slotted spoon, draining it well. Tip the liquor into a small pan and simmer gently until syrupy.

Release the cheesecake from its tin and place it on a serving plate. Arrange the rhubarb on top and brush with the hot syrup. Chill until set, about 30 minutes. Cut the cheesecake into slices to serve. It can be stored in a covered container in the fridge for up to 3–4 days, but remove about an hour before serving to bring to room temperature.

SERVES 12
CRUST:
115g digestive biscuits, crushed
1 tbsp caster sugar
50g unsalted butter, melted

FILLING:
100g white chocolate
900g cream cheese
grated zest of 1 lemon
1 tsp vanilla extract
150g caster sugar
4 medium eggs
450ml soured cream

TOPPING:
250g trimmed young rhubarb, rinsed
1 tbsp redcurrant jelly

A rich New York style baked cheesecake – flavoured with white chocolate, lemon zest and vanilla, and topped with a lightly cooked rhubarb glaze.

Alastair Hendy's
Swiss Chocolate Cake

8–12 SLICES
180g butter, plus extra to grease
210g shelled, skinned hazelnuts
20g plain flour
280g dark, bitter chocolate
   (minimum 70% cocoa solids),
   in pieces
200g caster sugar
6 medium eggs, separated

TO SERVE:
icing sugar
whipped whipping cream

Preheat the oven to 200°C/Gas 6. Grease a 24cm springform cake tin. Scatter the hazelnuts on a baking tray and roast in the oven for about 8 minutes until they smell lightly toasted. Tip onto a plate and allow to cool, then grind the nuts to fine crumbs and mix with the flour.

Put the chocolate in a heatproof bowl set over a pan of simmering water (making sure the water isn't in contact with the bowl) and leave until melted, then take off the heat.

Beat 130g of the sugar with the butter and egg yolks until pale and creamy. In another bowl, whisk the egg whites with the remaining sugar until stiff. Mix the melted chocolate with the egg yolk and sugar mixture, then gently mix the hazelnut flour mixture through this. Finally fold through the beaten egg whites.

Spoon the cake mixture into the prepared tin and bake for around 60–70 minutes. Allow to cool in the tin a little, then transfer to a wire rack and dust with icing sugar – don't fret if the cake sinks a little and cracks, it's all part of the charm. Eat slices tidal-waved with whipped cream.

Katrin's Schokoladenkuchen (that's chocolate cake to you) is big and gorgeous. Made daily at the Hotel Jungfrau – perched high up in the Swiss mountains in Wengernalp, it's a *kuchen* that *fraus* fight over, and all skiers lust after. All (massive) slices must come with a big dollop of whipped cream – it's the law.

Sophie Grigson's
Torta Caprese

SERVES 8–10

200g butter, melted and cooled
   until tepid, plus extra to grease
200g dark chocolate, in pieces
4 large eggs
170g caster sugar
1 tsp vanilla extract
250g ground almonds

TO SERVE:
raspberries or orange slices
   (optional)
icing sugar, to dust
few drops of rosewater (optional)
crème fraîche or whipped cream
   (optional)

Line the base of a 24cm cake tin with baking parchment and grease the sides. Preheat the oven to 180°C/Gas 4.

Whiz the chocolate in a food processor until finely chopped, but still retaining a little texture. If you don't have a processor, chop it finely with a large knife.

In a large bowl, beat the eggs with the sugar and vanilla extract until the sugar has dissolved. Mix in the chocolate, ground almonds and butter until evenly combined. Spoon the mixture into the prepared tin.

Bake for 50–60 minutes, until the cake is just firm to the touch. Leave to cool in the tin, then turn out.

If you are serving the cake with raspberries, put these in a bowl, sprinkle with a little icing sugar and the rosewater and leave to macerate for at least half an hour while the cake is cooling.

Dust the surface of the cake liberally with icing sugar. Serve cut into wedges, on its own, or with orange slices or raspberries and a dollop of crème fraîche or cream.

The easiest, lushest chocolate cake ever – dense, moist and mottled with nuggets of chocolate, it's more a pudding than a teatime cake … a winner every time. Serve it on its own, with double cream, or best of all with a scoop of crème fraîche and a handful of raspberries in the summer, or slices of mango or tangy orange during the winter.

Darina Allen's
Chocolate Meringue Cake

SERVES 10–12

4 egg whites
260g icing sugar
4 rounded tsp cocoa powder

CHOCOLATE WAFERS:
110g good quality dark chocolate

CHOCOLATE AND RUM CREAM:
75g good quality dark chocolate
2 tbsp dark rum
600ml double cream

Preheat the oven to 150°C/Gas 2. Line three baking sheets with silicone paper and mark a 23cm circle on each. Put the egg whites into a clean, dry bowl. Add 225g icing sugar and whisk until the mixture forms stiff, dry peaks, about 10 minutes. Sift the cocoa powder and remaining 35g icing sugar together and gently fold into the meringue.

Divide the meringue between the three prepared baking sheets and spread to cover the rounds with a palette knife. Immediately bake in the oven for 45 minutes or until just crisp. Turn off the oven and leave the meringue rounds inside to cool. When completely cold, remove and peel off the paper.

To make the chocolate wafers, melt the chocolate (see page 13) and spread on a sheet of silicone paper or light card. Leave in a cool place until firm enough to cut into squares or diamond shapes.

Meanwhile, make the chocolate and rum cream. Very gently melt the chocolate with the rum and 2 tbsp of the cream in a heatproof bowl set over a pan of simmering water. Remove from the heat and leave to cool. Whip the remaining cream until soft peaks form, then fold into the cooled chocolate mixture; don't overmix or it may curdle.

Sandwich the three meringue discs together with the chocolate and rum cream and decorate with chocolate wafers. For a special celebration, add sparklers if you like!

A luscious cake ... very naughty, but very nice!

Lounge Bar

As the day ebbs away and the dusk gives way to evening, you might well still have chocolate on your mind. So why not slip into something more comfortable and join us for a cocktail or two. Or if you prefer, we can tantalise your taste buds with exciting recipes embracing the warmth of chilli and the lively zest of fruit.

Hotel Chocolat's
Truffle Reviver

SERVES 2
2 Champagne chocolate truffles
75ml brandy
25ml apricot or cherry liqueur

Put each chocolate truffle into a shot glass. Then, in a saucepan, gently heat the brandy and liqueur together until warmed through (but not too hot to drink). Pour the liquor over the chocolates, ignite the brandy if you like with a taper and serve.

Fine quality truffles make all the difference to this cocktail. Use the richest, chocolate-coated truffles that you can find – definitely not ones that are coated in cocoa powder.

McRae's
Chocolate Cherry Cocktail

SERVES 2
60ml chocolate-flavoured liqueur
60ml cherry liqueur
60ml vodka
1 tbsp chocolate syrup

To Serve:
**fresh cherries or chocolate-dipped
cherries (optional)**

Fill a cocktail shaker with ice. Add the chocolate and cherry
liqueurs, and the vodka. Shake briskly to mix and chill. Drizzle
the chocolate syrup into two chilled martini glasses and strain in
the cocktail. Decorate with the cherries.

Sophisticated enough for the
smartest of occasions – a chocoholic's
dream tipple.

Rose Elliot's
Berry Skewers
with white chocolate sauce

MAKES 20

200g mixed berries (such as small strawberries, large blueberries, raspberries)

WHITE CHOCOLATE SAUCE:
100g white chocolate, in pieces
120ml double cream

To make the sauce, melt the chocolate (see page 13), then remove from the heat and stir in the cream. Put into a small serving bowl and set aside to cool.

Spear one or two berries onto each of 20 small wooden skewers or cocktail sticks – enough for a mouthful. Arrange the skewers around the bowl of dip and serve.

Minimum effort for maximum effect – so easy to do and yet so stunning. With soft fruit, chocolate and cream, you really can't lose...

Elegant chocolate-dipped strawberries are perfect sweet nibbles to serve at a cocktail party.

Sue McMahon's
Tuxedo Strawberries

MAKES 12–15
12–15 large strawberries (stalks intact)
150g white chocolate, melted
150g dark chocolate, melted

Line a tray with baking parchment. Dip each strawberry into the melted white chocolate to coat all of it except for the top, letting the excess drain off. Place the strawberries on the prepared tray and leave until the chocolate has set.

Holding the fruit by the stalk, dip one side of each strawberry into the melted dark chocolate, then dip the other side, leaving a 'V' of white chocolate in the centre. Allow the excess chocolate to drain off, then place the strawberries on the tray and leave them to set.

To decorate the dipped strawberries, if you like, spoon some dark chocolate into a small greaseproof paper piping bag and snip off the tip to give a small hole. Pipe a bow-tie onto the top of each strawberry and pipe 3 dots on each as buttons. Leave until the chocolate has set before serving.

Orlando Murrin's
Fresh Raspberry Truffles

MAKES 20–24

150g fresh raspberries (or frozen, defrosted and well drained)
125g dark chocolate, in pieces
4 tbsp double cream

15g butter
2 tsp maple syrup, honey or golden syrup
15g cocoa powder, sifted

Whiz the raspberries in a food processor to a purée, then pass through a sieve into a bowl to remove the seeds, pressing with a wooden spoon to extract all the liquid. Set aside.

Put the chocolate, cream, butter and syrup in a heatproof bowl. Set over a pan of gently simmering water and stir frequently until the chocolate has melted and the mixture is smooth and glossy. (Alternatively melt in a microwave for about 1 minute, then stir until smooth.)

Stir the raspberry purée into the melted chocolate mixture until evenly blended. Let cool and then refrigerate overnight, or until the mixture does not stick to your finger when pressed.

Now comes the messy (fun) bit. Put the cocoa powder into a shallow bowl. Scoop a generous teaspoonful of the chilled truffle mixture into your hands and roll it into a ball. Drop the ball into the cocoa. Do the same with another 4 balls. Roll the balls about gently in the cocoa with a spoon, then lift onto a plate lined with a piece of baking parchment.

Repeat with the rest of the mixture to make 20–24 truffles. Cover loosely with cling film and keep chilled. Serve straight from the fridge and eat within a week.

A light touch is needed to make these very soft, fresh-tasting truffles.

Devilishly good... so make these truffles in big batches and store in the freezer until you need them. Just don't leave them lying around – they're incredibly more-ish. Serve to round off a special meal, or pack into boxes and give as presents to friends. For more subtly spiced truffles, omit the chilli flakes.

Thomasina Miers'
Chilli Chocolate Truffles

SERVES LOTS!

vegetable oil, to oil tin
500g dark, bitter chocolate (about 70% cocoa solids)
200g dark chocolate (about 50% cocoa solids)
good pinch of ground allspice
good pinch of ground cinnamon

10 cloves
1 tsp dried chilli flakes
400ml double cream
30g butter
2 tbsp dark rum, whisky or brandy
50g cocoa powder

Lightly oil a 30 x 12cm baking tin (or tin with similar dimensions) and line with cling film. Break up the chocolate into a bowl. Grind the allspice, cinnamon, cloves and chilli flakes together, using a mortar and pestle.

Gently heat the cream and ground spices in a heavy-based pan until hot but not boiling. Add to the chocolate and stir through. If the chocolate has not melted completely, set the bowl over a pan of simmering water to warm gently and melt any last chunks. Stir in the butter and rum. Pour the mixture into the prepared tin and spread level. Freeze for 1 hour.

To finish, sift the cocoa powder into a large bowl. Carefully turn the chocolate truffle out onto a board, remove the cling film and cut into 2–3cm cubes. Toss gently in the cocoa powder. Store in a plastic bag in the freezer until required.

Jenny Chandler's
Chocolate Toasties
with olive oil and rock salt

SERVES 4

50g dark chocolate (minimum
   70% cocoa solids)
4 small slices of good white
   country bread

extra virgin olive oil
rock salt, to sprinkle
cocoa powder, sifted, to sprinkle
   (optional)

Preheat the oven to 180°C/Gas 4. Break the chocolate into 4 even chunks and place one on each slice of bread. Lay on a baking sheet and warm through in the oven for 5 minutes, or until the chocolate just begins to melt.

Drizzle with extra virgin olive oil, and sprinkle with rock salt and a little sifted cocoa powder if you like. Serve at once.

Fabulous, but unlikely combination from the Estrella de Plata Bar in Barcelona. It's all about using top quality ingredients — choose a really delicious bitter chocolate and fine extra virgin olive oil.

Amanda Grant's
Hot Chocolate

SERVES 4

100g dark or milk chocolate (or
  half of each), in pieces
600ml full-fat milk (or semi-
  skimmed if you prefer)

75ml double cream, softly
  whipped
8 marshmallows (optional)
a little cocoa powder, to dust

Melt the chocolate slowly over a pan of simmering water (see page 13). Take off the heat and give the chocolate a gentle stir with a wooden spoon until it is smooth and glossy.

Heat the milk gently in a saucepan until it is about to boil, but don't let it actually boil. Remove from the heat and pour a little onto the chocolate, stirring constantly with a whisk until you have a thick paste. Pour on the rest of the milk, whisking as you do so, until the mixture is slightly frothy.

Carefully pour into mugs and spoon the whipped cream on top. Finish with the marshmallows and a sprinkling of cocoa.

A smooth, comforting hot chocolate drink, which is equally delicious cold – just let it cool, then serve poured over ice, or topped with a scoop of ice cream. Instead of cocoa powder, sprinkle with grated chocolate or a small pinch of ground cinnamon.

Fiona Beckett's
Ultimate Cocoa

MAKES 1 MUG
2 tsp cocoa powder
4 tbsp Baileys cream liqueur
1 tbsp Kahlua or Tia Maria
   (optional but good)
about 200ml semi-skimmed milk

Quite simply this has to be the best cocoa ever!

Put the cocoa powder in a mug. Add the Baileys, and Kahlua if using, and stir well. Top up with milk and stir. Microwave for 1 minute, stir again, then microwave for a further 30 seconds or until warmed to your liking. Stir and indulge!

Angus Thirlwell's
Purist's Hot Chocolate

The essential ingredient is a cocoa stick – a fat cigar-shaped roll made only with roasted cocoa nibs. These are available at Hotel Chocolat and at street markets in the West Indies and Latin America.

Using a fine cheese grater, begin grating the cocoa stick. Allow 5 tsp per 225ml mug serving. Add to a pan of 50:50 mixed semi-skimmed milk and water (allowing 200ml per serving). Simmer for 10 minutes, stirring continuously. Pass the chocolate through a sieve to remove the residual pieces of cocoa nib.

There will be spots of melted cocoa butter on the surface, but don't be concerned. This is natural, as this drink is made from the whole cocoa bean and the butter has not been separated out (unlike with cocoa powder). Sweeten with sugar if you like, to serve.

You can vary this recipe by infusing the milk with other flavourings. Try adding 1 bay leaf and ½ tsp each of freshly grated nutmeg and cinnamon (per 2 mugs) at the beginning of the simmering stage.

An invigorating, powerful brew that harnesses all the power of the cocoa bean – great if you are planning to party long into the night. Prepared the same way as the Elizabethans would have taken it in early chocolate houses in London, the taste is as authentic as it gets.

Index

Acknowledgements

Copyright belongs to the author unless stated otherwise below. The recipe copyright holder is listed first, the photography copyright holder is listed second, after / . **Note:** all photographs by Vanessa Courtier are © Hotel Chocolat 2007.

PRELIMS AND INTRODUCTION
p.1 Vanessa Courtier; pp.4–5 images repeated from recipe pages; p.7 Food Features; pp.8 & 9 Vanessa Courtier; p.11 Hotel Chocolat; p.12 Vanessa Courtier; p.14 Vanessa Courtier. Introductory text by Jane Suthering, 2007.

THE RECIPES
pp.16–17 photo by Stephen Bond for Hotel Chocolat;
pp.18–19 Jane Suthering / Debbie Patterson;
p.20 © Felicity Barnum-Bobb 2006/ © Steve Baxter and Marie-Louise Avery 2006 (from *100 Magnificent Muffins & Scones* by Felicity Barnum-Bobb, published by HarperCollins Publishers Ltd, 2006), reprinted by permission of HarperCollins Publishers Ltd;
p.21 Christine France / Don Last;
pp.22–23 Jacque Malouf / Tara Fisher, text and photo © Conran Octopus 2005 (from *Breakfasts*, published by Conran Octopus Limited, 2005), reproduced by permission of Conran Octopus Limited;
p.24 words by Jennie Milsom / photo by Martin Thompson, Good Housekeeping (UK), © The National Magazine Company Limited;
p.25 Sue Lawrence / Jean Cazals;
pp.26–27 Eric Treuille and Ursula Ferrigno / DK Images;
pp.28–29 © Richard Bertinet 2005 / © Jean Cazals 2005 (from *Dough* by Richard Bertinet, published by Kyle Cathie Limited, 2005);
pp.30–31 Mary Norwak / Vanessa Courtier;
pp.32–33 photo by Stephen Bond for Hotel Chocolat;
pp.34–35 recipe and photo © Australian Women's Weekly *Chocolate: 70 Wicked Recipes* (ACP Books);
pp.36–37 "Hazelnut and chocolate chunk cookies" from *A Passion for Puddings* by Phil Vickery, photography by Steve Baxter, published by Simon & Shuster UK Ltd, 2005 (text and photo © Société Des Produits Nestlé, 2005), author photo by permission of Phil Vickery;
p.38 Constance Spry (based on a recipe from *The Constance Spry Cookery Book* by Constance Spry and Rosemary Hume, published by J.M Dent & Sons Ltd, 1956) / Vanessa Courtier;
p.39 Michael Caines / Vanessa Courtier;
pp.40–41 Mitzie Wilson / Michael Paul;
p.42 "Chocolate Crispies" by Mary Berry from *Foolproof Cakes* published by BBC Books. Reprinted by permission of The Random House Group Ltd / photo © Jean Cazals 2004;
p.43 recipe and photo © Australian Women's Weekly *Chocolate: 70 Wicked Recipes* (ACP Books);
pp.44–45 recipe and photos © Australian Women's Weekly *Chocolate: 70 Wicked Recipes* (ACP Books);
pp.46–47 Anna Del Conte (from *Gastronomy of Italy* by Anna Del Conte, revised edition published by Pavilion Books, 2004), recipe photograph by Tim Hill, author photo by permission of Seven Publishing;
p.48 © Jill Norman 2005 / © Jason Lowe 2005 (from *Winter Food* by Jill Norman, published by Kyle Cathie Limited, 2005);
p.49 Jeremy Lee / Peter Williams;
pp.50–51 Jane Suthering / Debbie Patterson;
p.52 Paul Hollywood (from *100 Great Breads* by Paul Hollywood, published by Cassell Illustrated, 2004), photo by Neil Barclay;
p.53 recipe and photo © Glynn Christian;
pp.54–55 photo by Stephen Bond for Hotel Chocolat;
pp.56–57 Lynda Brown / Vanessa Courtier;
pp.58–59 Aiden Byrne / Vanessa Courtier (recipe photo and author photo);
p.60 recipe and photo © McRae Books Srl 2005 (from *The Chocolate Cookbook*);
p.61 Jenny Chandler / Vanessa Courtier;
pp.62–63 Joanna Farrow / Vanessa Courtier;
pp.64–65 Elizabeth Luard (from *The Latin American Kitchen*, published by Kyle Cathie Limited, 2006) / Vanessa Courtier;
p.66 Matthew Fort / Vanessa Courtier;
p.67 Joanna Farrow / Vanessa Courtier;
pp.68–69 Lindsey Bareham / Vanessa Courtier;
pp.70–71 Carol Wilson / Billington's Unrefined Sugars;
pp.72–73 Prue Leith / Vanessa Courtier, author photo by Paul Tozer;
pp.74–75 Charles Campion / Vanessa Courtier;
pp.76–77 photo by Stephen Bond for Hotel Chocolat;
p.78 Alex Barker / Food Features;
p.79 Diana Henry / Vanessa Courtier;
p.80 Kate Whiteman / Vanessa Courtier;
p.81 recipe and photo © Australian Women's Weekly *Chocolate: 70 Wicked Recipes* (ACP Books);
pp.82–83 Annie Bell / Chris Alack;
p.84 recipe and photo © Australian Women's Weekly *Chocolate: 70 Wicked Recipes* (ACP Books);
p.85 Mary Gwynn / William Reavell;
pp.86–87 Galton Blackiston / photo by permission of Navigator Guides (from *A Return to Real Cooking* by Galton Blackiston, published by Navigator Guides, 2006);
p.88 Joanna Farrow / Vanessa Courtier;
p.89 Sarah Jane Evans / Vanessa Courtier;

pp.90–91 Anne Willan / Langdon Clay;
pp.92–93 based on an original by Michael Smith / Vanessa Courtier;
pp.94–95 Alex Mackay / Peter Knabb (from *Cooking in Provence* by Alex Mackay, published by Ebury Press, back in print April 2008);
pp.96–97 recipe reproduced by permission of Bryan and Joyce Round / Vanessa Courtier;
pp.98–99 © Tamasin Day-Lewis 2004 (from *Tamasin's Weekend Food*, published by Weidenfeld & Nicolson, 2004) / Vanessa Courtier, author photo by permission of Weidenfeld & Nicolson, an imprint of The Orion Publishing Group Ltd;
pp.100–101 Jane Suthering / Debbie Patterson;
pp.102–103 Marie Pierre Moine / Vanessa Courtier;
pp.104–105 recipe and photo © Patrick Anthony;
pp.106–107 Henrietta Green and Josceline Dimbleby / Jess Koppel;
pp.108–109 Angela Nilsen / William Lingwood (recipe and photo reproduced by permission of *BBC Good Food Magazine*);
pp.110–111 Marguerite Patten / Vanessa Courtier, author photo by permission of Marguerite Patten;
pp.112–3 Hugo Arnold / Georgia Glynn Smith (from the *Avoca Café Cookbook* by Hugo Arnold with Lesley Hayes, 2000);
pp.114–5 photo by Stephen Bond for Hotel Chocolat;
pp.116–7 recipe and photo by permission of The Pudding Club;
pp.118–9 Michel Roux / Martin Brigdale, author photo by Martin Brigdale;
p.120 based on an original by Mrs Beeton / Vanessa Courtier;
p.121 Sarah Edington / Anova Books Ltd (from the *Complete Traditional Recipe Book* by Sarah Edington, published by National Trust Books, 2006), recipe and photo reproduced by permission of Anova Books Company Ltd;
p.122–3 Henrietta Green / Jason Lowe;
p.124 Bea Harling / Nick Carman;
p.125 Frank Bordoni / Anna Ahktar;
pp.126–7 "Dark Mocha Soufflés" by Mary Cadogan from *Good Food Magazine: Dangerous Desserts*, published by BBC Books. Reprinted by permission of The Random House Group Ltd; photo © Martin Brigdale;
pp.128–9 "Tarte Belle Helene" from *The French Market* by Fran Warde and Joanne Harris, published by Transworld. Reprinted by permission of The Random House Group Ltd / photo by Debi Treloar, reproduced by permission of The Random House Group Ltd;
pp.130–1 © Ed Baines 2001 / © Gus Filgate 2001 (from *Entertain* by Ed Baines, published by Kyle Cathie Limited, 2001);
pp.132–3 Terry Laybourne / Duncan Davis (from *Terry Laybourne's Quest for Taste*, published by Quest for Taste Publishing, 2004);
pp.134–5 recipe and photos © Anton Mosimann;
p.136 Tonia George / photo by Mark Roper for *Waitrose Food Illustrated* magazine;
p.137 text and photo © Rosemary Moon;
p.138 text and photo © Murdoch Books 2006 (from *Cooking from Scratch* by Lulu Grimes, published by Murdoch Books, 2006);
p.139 Celia Brooks Brown / Jan Baldwin;
pp.140–1 "Chocolate Parfait with Summer Berries" from Antony Worrall Thompson's *Weekend Cookbook*, photography by Steve Lee, published by BBC Books. Text and photo reproduced by permission of The Random House Group Ltd. Author photo by Nick Ayliffe;
pp.142–3 Linda Tubby / Peter Cassidy;
p.144 Mark Hix / Jason Lowe;
p.145 text and photo © Jill Dupleix;
pp.146–7 Robin Weir / Vanessa Courtier;
pp.148–9 Mark Hix / Jason Lowe, author photo by Jason Lowe;
p.150 text and photo © Grub Street Publishing (from *Chocolate, the Definitive Guide* by Sara Jayne Stanes, published by Grub Street, 1999);
p.151 Lyn Hall / Vanessa Courtier;
pp.152–3 Mary Berry / Juliet Piddington (from *Real Food – Fast* published by Headline Book Publishing, 2005);
pp.154–5 Paul and Jeanne Rankin / Gus Filgate;
p.156 Peter Gordon / Jean Cazals;
p.157 Jane Suthering / Steve Baxter;
pp.158–9 text and photo © Grace Mulligan;
pp.160–61 Linda Collister / Anthony Blake;
pp.162–3 text and photo © Alastair Hendy;
pp.164–5 Sophie Grigson / Georgia Glynn Smith; author photo reproduced by permission of Sophie Grigson;
pp.166–7 © Darina Allen 2005 / © Peter Cassidy 2005 (from *Easy Entertaining* by Darina Allen, published by Kyle Cathie Limited, 2005);
pp.168–9 photo by Stephen Bond for Hotel Chocolat;
p.170 Jane Suthering / Vanessa Courtier;
p.171 recipe and photo © McRae Books Srl 2005 (from *The Chocolate Cookbook*);
p.172 © Rose Elliot 2006 / photo by Jason Lowe © Hamlyn 2006 (from *Veggie Chic* by Rose Elliot, published by Hamlyn, 2006);
p.173 text and photo © Woman's Weekly/IPC+Syndication;
p.174 Orlando Murrin / Jason Lowe;
p.175 © Thomasina Miers 2006 / photo by Noel Murphy © HarperCollins 2006 (from *Cook* by Thomasina Miers, published by Collins, 2006), reprinted by permission of HarperCollins Publishers Ltd;
p.176 Jenny Chandler / Jean Cazals;
p.177 Amanda Grant / Vanessa Courtier;
p.178 Fiona Beckett / Vanessa Courtier;
p.179 Angus Thirlwell / Stephen Bond (© Hotel Chocolat 2007).

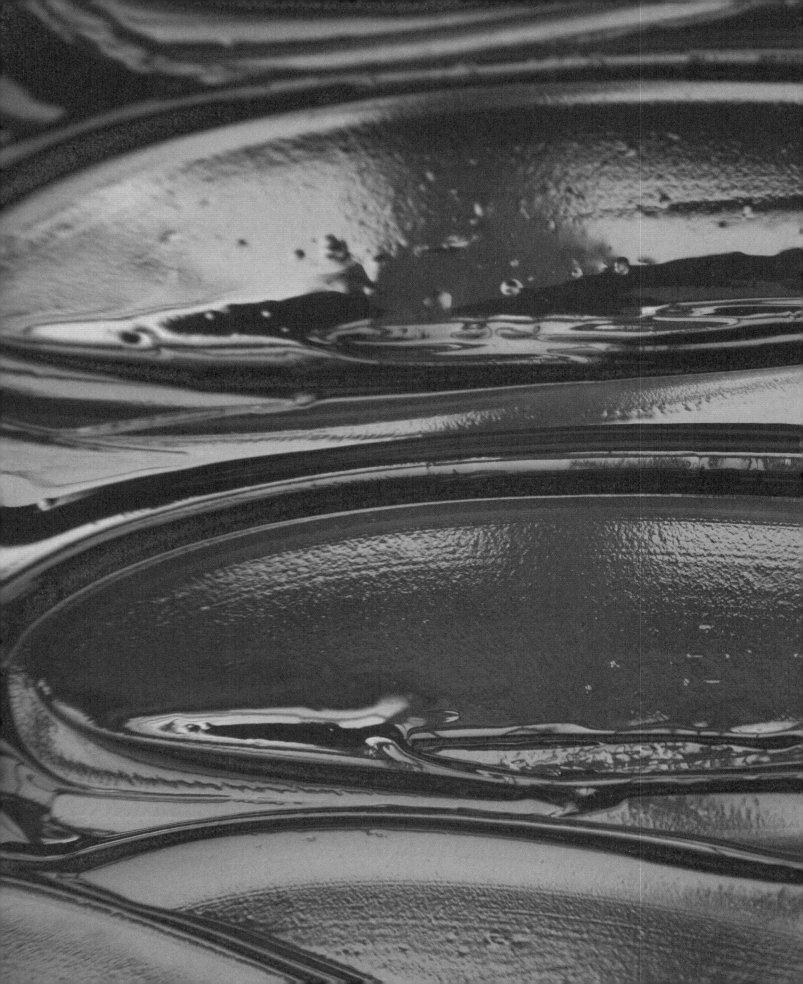